17-
ᴇᴅ

MW00583486

# SIGMUND FREUD:

*Man and Father*

# COMMENTARY

Sigmund Freud (1856-1939) had six children: Matilde, Martin, and Oliver, born when the family lived in the Suehnhaus, and Ernst, Sophie, and Anna, who were born in the apartment at Bergasse 19. This book, by his oldest son Martin, is an unpretentious memoir—a collection of reminiscences of family activities—without discussion of Freud's monumental contribution of man's knowledge of himself.

Here you'll find grandma Amalia (Freud's mother) who, on the far side of 90 years of age, could say while trying on hats, "I won't take this one; it makes me look old." It is full of such probably irrelevant facts as Freud's favorite dish (boiled beef), his dislikes (telephones and bicycles), and his angry comment, when a 4-year-old grandson wandered down the street and cranked the engine of a motor vehicle, that there was not the slightest sense in becoming attached to a boy who must sooner or later kill himself in dangerous escapades. It also covers his last week in Vienna under Nazi occupation and subsequent escape to England.

# SIGMUND FREUD:

## *Man and Father*

by Martin Freud

Jason Aronson/New York and London

# INTRODUCTION
*by H.R.H. the Princess George of Greece*

I WENT to Vienna in 1925 to undergo an analysis by Professor Freud, and in subsequent years I spent several months
and weeks in Vienna for the same purpose. I thus had the
occasion to make the acquaintance of his family, and could
witness the harmonious atmosphere of that home—until, in
1938, Hitler destroyed so much happiness.

Martin Freud, the author of this book, I have known for
thirty years. The eldest son of Freud, he was, as he says himself
in this book, put in charge of the *Verlag,* the publishing firm
his father had created. I often met him as such and also in the
family circle. I could then appreciate fully his lively personality, his youthful humour, which never deserted him in the
most difficult circumstances, and which the passage of time has
not dimmed in the least, as the reader of this book can witness.

Martin evokes in all its freshness the childhood impressions
of the lively boy he was in the wake of his great father, their
holidays in the mountains, all fragrant with the scent of wild
strawberries and of those large mushrooms (Herrenpilze) his
father was so fond of discovering under the great fir-trees of
the forests he so much loved.

He also lets us watch him growing up, choosing his career
under the guidance of such a father—and his book is sprinkled
with delightful anecdotes, notably that of the "Astrologer and
Psychoanalyst" who pestered his father with letters. Wearing
a large beard, wig and appropriately disguised, Martin imper-
sonated the "Astrologer and Psychoanalyst" and called on his
father.

We enjoy with him mountaineering experiences and suffer
accidents with him, and with him we watch several of the
important political events of those times. He fought in the
First World War and won a well-deserved Military Cross as an
officer in the Austrian army. We read of the Austrian invasion
of Poland, the war in Italy, the Armistice, and his months of

captivity. We are told of the two Austrian civil wars and finally of the terrible days of Hitler's invasion of Austria, when Hitler destroyed the peace and charm of the Vienna I had myself known for so many years, full of mirth, music and, for those who lived in Freud's atmosphere, of the serenity of scientific research.

Most of Freud's pupils and associates, who had formed the Viennese Psychoanalytical Society, were dispersed as formerly the Berlin group had been scattered. Some went to America, others to England, where, in June 1938, Freud himself, with his family, took refuge, welcomed by all.

While Anna, the youngest of his children, was the only one to follow in her father's footsteps, and became an eminent analyst, Martin remained for his father in exile the devoted son he always had been and I could at each of my visits to the Freuds in London meet him at his father's home, as I also met his brother Ernst, the architect, and Mathilde, the eldest daughter of Freud.

I knew of Martin's intention to write a book about his youthful remembrances and of the eventful years that followed. I am happy to see that he has realized this purpose, and I wish the readers of his book as much pleasure in reading it as I had myself, and as Martin himself, I doubt not, had in recalling to life these souvenirs of a distant but always vivid past.

MARIE BONAPARTE

# SIGMUND FREUD:

## *Man and Father*

# CHAPTER I

I BEGIN this story a few days after the end of the Sigmund Freud centenary celebrations in London. The last lectures and broadcasts have been given to mark the occasion, as the last articles have been written. Many came to admire and revere, some came to criticize, and there were frank unbelievers; but no one denied that my father was a genius.

The human race is not densely sprinkled with persons of genius: each is a rare phenomenon. To have a genius for a father is not a common experience: in consequence, as Sigmund Freud's eldest son, I am a member of a small minority, the object of some curiosity, but not necessarily looked upon with much favour by society. Society is not, it would seem, prepared to cheer loudly when any one of us tries to climb to fame and glory. Personally, I make no complaint. I have never had any ambition to rise to eminence, although, I must admit, I have been quite happy and content to bask in reflected glory. Nevertheless, I believe that if the son of a great and famous father wants to get anywhere in this world he must follow the advice given to Alice by the Red Queen —he will have to go twice as fast if he does not want to stop where he is. The son of a genius remains the son of a genius, and his chances of winning human approval of anything he may do hardly exist if he attempts to make any claim to a fame detached from that of his father.

I know something of psychoanalysis, and I firmly believe in my father's theories; but I do not feel called upon to explain them here. The Sigmund Freud about whom I am writing is not the celebrated scientist in his study or mounted on the lecture rostrum; he is my gay and generous father in the circle of his family, perhaps at home, perhaps tramping with his children through the forests, fishing from a rowing-boat on an alpine lake, or climbing mountains.

May I be allowed here to make a short excursion back into the past to tell something about my father's and my mother's childhood, about their parents, and about their brothers and sisters?

I cannot hope to give many new facts about them. All I can do is to add my own personal memories of those who played parts in my family history.

My father was born on 6th May 1856 in the Moravian town of Freiberg, a very old and rather small industrial town which then belonged to the Austro-Hungarian Empire. His mother, Amalia, was the second wife of his father, Jakob Freud, who was born in 1815; and she was twenty years his junior. The result was a curious one, because Jakob's children by his first wife were already grown up and one of them, Emanuel, was married and had children. He, Emanuel, was some years older than his step-mother Amalia and lived in the immediate neighbourhood. My father was the uncle of his first playmate, Emanuel's son, a year older than himself.

When my father was about four years old, Jakob Freud, whose small textile firm was declining with Freiberg's industrial importance, decided to liquidate his business. With his young wife and their two children, Sigmund and Anna, he left Moravia and eventually settled in Vienna. Emanuel, incidentally, emigrated to England and succeeded in establishing himself in Manchester in his father's textile trade.

I knew Jakob, Amalia and Emanuel. I was seven years old when my grandfather died and I can recall him quite clearly, because he was a frequent visitor to our Vienna flat then in the Bergasse. Every member of my family loved Jakob and treated him with great respect. He was tall and broad-shouldered, very much the size to which I reached when I grew up myself. He was terribly nice with us children. He brought us small presents and he used to tell us stories, mostly with a little twinkle in his great brown eyes, as if he wanted to say, "Isn't everything we are doing and saying here a great joke?"

When he died, in October 1896, my father wrote to his friend, Dr Fliess: "By one of the dark ways behind the official consciousness, my father's death has affected me profoundly. I had treasured him highly and had understood him exactly. With his peculiar mixture of deep wisdom and fantastic lightness he had meant very much in my life. . . ."

I saw my Grandmother Amalia often. Although she was an old woman when, as a small boy, I became conscious of her, I was already a middle-aged man when she died. She had had great beauty, but all traces of this had gone when I remember her first. It looked for some time as if she would live for ever, and my father was terrified by the thought that she might survive him and, in consequence, have to be told of his death.

Grandmother came from East Galicia, then still part of the Austrian Empire. She came of Jewish stock; and it might not be known by many people that Galician Jews were a peculiar race, not only different from any other races inhabiting Europe, but absolutely different from Jews who had lived in the West for some generations. They, these Galician Jews, had little grace and no manners; and their women were certainly not what we should call "ladies". They were highly emotional and easily carried away by their feelings. But, although in many respects they would seem to be untamed barbarians to more civilized people, they, alone of all minorities, stood up against the Nazis. It was men of Amalia's race who fought the German army on the ruins of Warsaw; and it might, indeed, be true to say that whenever you hear of Jews showing violence or belligerence, instead of that meekness and what seems poor-spirited acceptance of a hard fate sometimes associated with Jewish peoples, you may safely suspect the presence of men and women of Amalia's race.

These people are not easy to live with, and grandmother, a true representative of her race, was no exception. She had great vitality and much impatience; she had a hunger for life and an indomitable spirit. Nobody envied Aunt Dolfi, whose destiny it was to dedicate her life to the care of an old mother who was a tornado. Aunt Dolfi once took Amalia to buy a new hat—and she was not perhaps wise to recommend what seemed to her "something suitable". Studying carefully her image crowned by the hat she had agreed to try on, Amalia, who was on the wrong side of ninety, finally shouted, "I won't take this one; it makes me look old."

Memorable occasions were the family gatherings in Amalia's flat. These were on Christmas Day and New Year's Eve, for Amalia ignored Jewish feasts. The meals showed opulence; we were usually offered roast goose, candied fruits, cakes and punch

—the last-named being in a weakened form for us children. When I was young, my Uncle Alexander was still unmarried, and he took charge of the entertainment side of the gatherings. He was the heart and soul of the parties. He arranged games so that they were played in order, and poems, written for each occasion, were recited and given full applause.

But always, as the evening went on, an atmosphere of growing crisis was felt by all as Amalia became unsettled and anxious. There are people who, when they are unsettled and disturbed, will hide these feelings because they do not want to affect the peace of those around them; but Amalia was not one of these. My father always came to these gatherings—I know of no occasion when he disappointed her—but his working day was a long one and he always came much later than any one else. Amalia knew this, but perhaps it was a reality she could never accept. Soon she would be seen running anxiously to the door and out to the landing to stare down the staircase. Was he coming? Where was he? Was it not getting very late? This running in and out might go on for an hour, but it was known that any attempt to stop her would produce an outburst of anger which it was better to avoid by taking as little notice as possible. And my father always came at very much his usual time, but never at a moment when Amalia was waiting for him on the landing.

I can only recall my Uncle Emanuel, my father's half-brother; as a very old man. He was born in 1832, and was fifty-seven years older than myself. He, as I have said, emigrated to England, to Manchester, where he established himself in the textile trade. Now here is a peculiar thing. Uncle Emanuel, as the son of Jakob Freud, the small and not successful textile merchant of Freiberg in Moravia, had no importance, social or otherwise, when he reached Manchester. But when, in 1913, I went from Vienna to stay with him for a short holiday, I found him living in a large and comfortable house in Southport. This might be natural enough in a man who by hard work and ability had won wealth, but what has struck me since, after living in England for eighteen years and meeting British people in many walks of life, is the fact that Uncle Emanuel had become in every possible detail a digni-fied English gentleman. Indeed, while I have been received in many English homes, I have never enjoyed one that seemed so

Sigmund Freud's birthplace in Freiberg, Moravia

The "Suehnhaus" (House of Atonement) in Vienna, where Sigmund
Freud's first three children were born

Sigmund Freud at the age of eight with his father Jakob

Oliver, Martin and Ernst, the three sons of Sigmund Freud

typically English as that of my Uncle Emanuel at Southport; and this applies to his dress, his manners and his hospitality. I am not British by birth, and it is true that what seemed the important years of my life were spent in Austria, and that, in consequence, there may have been aspects of Uncle Emanuel's behaviour and *ménage* that betrayed the mid-European and escaped my attention; but I beg to doubt this. My impression of Uncle Emanuel's metamorphosis was gained when he, then about eighty, had retired from business and had left his control to his son Sam.

I have earlier memories, also, of Uncle Emanuel. During my youth in Vienna, being very fond of his half-brother (my father), Uncle Emanuel came to see us occasionally, events I recall because of the presents he bought us children. He liked to spend money, but he hated to waste it. In consequence, the selection of the presents was always a great and highly methodical occasion in which the cost of the gift was of much less importance than its uses or entertainment value. He was very fond of me, because I was the eldest son of his well-loved brother, but life with him was not easy. My father allowed his children to follow their own ideas of amusing themselves without paternal interference; but not so Uncle Emanuel. I recall that at Southport one day I wanted to go out in a rowing-boat when uncle decided that I should ride on a merry-go-round, something I disliked. The result of the long argument was that I did neither.

And, finally, something about my mother's ancestry. She came from a family of intellectuals. Two of her uncles were well-known men of letters and her grandfather had been the Chief Rabbi of Hamburg, a personage who had gained historical importance amongst the Jewish people of that city, where he was known as *cochem*, the wise one. His picture—I own a copy of the etching— shows an impressive philosopher's face. Born in Hamburg, my mother came at an early age to Vienna with her parents and her sister Minna.

Grandmother Emmeline was a much less vital personage than Amalia, but to us she was a character, too, and I remember her fairly well. She was an orthodox Jewess, a practising one, who hated and despised gay Vienna. True to the severe regulations of the orthodox Jewish law, she wore the *Scheitel*, which meant that at her marriage she had sacrificed her own hair, her head being crowned with two close-fitting artificial plaits. She stayed with us occasionally, and on Saturdays we used to hear her singing Jewish prayers in a small but firm and melodious voice. All of this, strangely enough in a Jewish family, seemed alien to us children who had been brought up without any instruction in Jewish ritual.

But although Grandmother Emmeline looked mild, soft and angelically sweet, she was always determined to have her own way. I remember the day when we were all out on some family errand and were caught in a terrific rainstorm. Following the motto "Old People and Children First", our parents put grandmother and a good handful of children into the only available carriage and sent us home. Since this was a one-horse conveyance, and very small, we were all packed as tightly as sardines in a tin and, because the small windows were shut, the air soon became very close and almost suffocating. We children wanted them opened; grandmother wanted them kept shut because of the rain; and at once a battle began between a handful of sturdy little brats and a frail old lady. The brats were no match for the lady—the windows remained shut. It was a miracle that we were all still alive when the carriage arrived home.

To complete the family story of the seven children of my Grandfather Jakob and my Grandmother Amalia, I cannot do better than to show here a reproduction of a picture—painted in oils—that hung in my grandmother's drawing-room. The original, with so many other family treasures, was lost in the Nazi invasion. The picture was painted nearly ninety years ago; therefore none of the persons shown remains alive. I could not find out the name of the painter, but it is unlikely that he ever became famous. I had better invent a little story and assume that he was some young man who had enjoyed hospitality in Jakob's house and had painted the group to show his gratitude, Jakob meeting the cost of the canvas and oils.

It would seem that the painter was only beginning to learn to paint, that he had learnt to do heads very nicely and would, in time, discover how to paint bodies and limbs. This will explain the comic lack of proportion which shows the children with big heads and stiff little bodies like dolls. The flowers the girls carry

may have been inspired by one of the great Viennese portrait artists, Waldmueller, for instance. However, that unknown
painter knew how to catch a likeness remarkably. We children of
Sigmund had no difficulty in identifying each child in the middle-
aged aunt it had grown into. I do hope the children, grandchildren and great-grandchildren of the now deceased ladies in
the picture will forgive my statement that none of the girls was
good-looking. In contrast, it will be agreed, I think, that Sigmund
is not only good-looking but even beautiful. I remember father
one day making a little joke at a moment when we were all looking at the picture. "The painter," he said, "has graciously overlooked the holes in the soles of my shoes." This was perhaps a
reference to the poverty of his youth.

The closing scenes in the lives of the five little girls in the picture, with the exception of Anna, the eldest, hardly bear thinking
about today. Anna, of a gay, happy temperament, truly a
Viennese, married my mother's brother, Eli Bernays, and died in
New York at the age of ninety-seven in peace and comfort surrounded by her adoring children. The other four little girls were
less fortunate.

Rosa, the next in age, married a prominent lawyer in Vienna
and lived for a time in a flat on the same floor we occupied at
Bergasse 19. She was my father's favourite sister, winning affection by great charm, much grace and dignity. People used to
compare her with the famous actress Eleanora Duse. I think she
was seventy before she lost her first tooth. As a widow, well on in
her sixties, she could still command love from young men, something about which she was very proud and not in the least discreet. But shadows began falling around her when she lost her
highly gifted children and when, to make more emphatic her
loneliness, she became totally deaf. Finally, she was murdered by
the Nazis, probably in Auschwitz.

That is one short statement to which the history of European
man during the last sixteen years has given the quality of the
commonplace; but it carries a world of degradation, a sordid unreality of hard reality. *Finally, she was murdered by the Nazis,
probably in Auschwitz.* One's mind pictures the awful physical
discomfort amidst foul odours and a starvation diet, until there
is created in the mind of an old woman used to normal comfort

something beyond indignation, a living sleepless death, drifting slowly but mercifully to endless sleep. Time has softened the impact of these hard events; but dare we forget that human beings could do just that to an old woman, and many thousands of other old women?

This makes me recall in particular my father's youngest sister, the smallest little girl in the picture, Dolfi, who, as I have said, dedicated her life to looking after Amalia, her mother. She was not clever or in any way remarkable, and it might be true to say that constant attendance on Amalia had suppressed her personality into a condition of dependence from which she never recovered. Alone of my father's sisters, she did not marry. Perhaps this made her somewhat unusual and subjective to impressions, or forebodings, of coming disasters which we thought ridiculous and even a little silly. I remember walking with her one day in Vienna when we passed an ordinary kind of man, probably a Gentile, who, so far as I knew, had taken no notice of us. I put it down to a pathological phobia, or Dolfi's stupidity, when she gripped my arm in terror and whispered, "Did you hear what that man said? He called me a dirty stinking Jewess and said it was time we were all killed."

At that time most of my own friends were Gentiles, and I felt perfectly happy and secure with them. It seems strange that while none of us—professors, lawyers and people of education— had any idea of the tragedy which would destroy the children of the Jewish race, a lovable but rather silly old maid foresaw, or appeared to foresee, that future. Dolfi herself died of starvation in the Jewish ghetto in Theresienstadt. The three other sisters were murdered, most probably at Auschwitz. Thus it was that four of the old sisters of my father, four of the little girls in the picture, suffered grievously in their last days.

There remains only to tell the story of the little boy with the doll and the whip in the picture. He was Alexander, ten years younger than my father, for whom there was no money to meet the cost of a university education. At a comparatively early age he had to abandon his studies to earn a living; but even without a university degree and consequent disadvantages, he went far. He became Austria's leading expert on transport. He was the consultant to the Vienna Chamber of Commerce on this subject and a professor at several academies. Finally he was made a counsellor (*kaiserlicher Rat*). He won the approbation of the Government for his services on transport problems during the First World War.

But he did not win the affection of the Vienna cabmen, for a very simple reason. An expert on transport costs, he applied his knowledge with much precision when he took an *Einspaenner*, perhaps to go from his office to my father's flat in the Bergasse. The Vienna city authorities had established a basic rate for the hiring of *Einspaenners*, calculated on the distance between different postal districts. This allowed the driver to charge for additional baggage, for extra passengers, for a dog or a cat, and for any waits while a passenger alighted, maybe to do some shopping. Uncle's journey to our flat was a lone expedition which could legally command only the basic fare no Viennese would ever dare to offer. But Uncle Alexander, otherwise generous and kindly, regarded transport in a purely scientific light which might not be dimmed by any nonsense in the way of faint-hearted appeasement; the result was a battle at the end of each journey, a combat that delighted us as we watched from our flat windows.

Uncle Alexander always won, but his series of victories, utterly shocking to the Viennese cabmen used to dealing with the good-tempered and placid inhabitants, became so famous that once, when he briskly approached a rank of *Einspaenners*, their drivers whipped up their horses, dispersed in a gallop and, it was said, have never been seen since. The fact that they were dealing with a transport expert of mid-European fame (who could not be swindled even in the most charming way) meant nothing to them.

Two brothers, my father and Alexander, could not have been more different in their outlook on life, but they were always good friends. In great contrast to Sigmund, Alexander was highly musical; indeed he could whistle in perfect tune a whole opera. In addition, he was an excellent story-teller who could imitate the various accents of the characters in his stories. Some might be ordinary Austrians, some were Jews from distant parts of the empire, others could be foreigners handling our language with more care than ability; but, however they spoke, Uncle

Alexander caught their accent. He came often to the Bergasse, and before he had a son of his own he spent many Sundays with the sons of his brother.

And that is a rough outline of the stories of the children in the picture painted so long ago.

# CHAPTER II

I WILL not deal with what is known of my father's very early childhood, up to the age of four. These stories have suffered much psychoanalytical interpretation. All I imagine is that, on the whole, my father was a well-behaved, healthy and sturdy boy, completely normal, who deeply loved both his father and mother and romped in high spirits with his playmates.

Undoubtedly, the removal from the pretty Moravian town of Freiberg with its rural surroundings to the far from clean and overcrowded Jewish quarter of Vienna, the Leopoldstadt, was, after the first excitement of the change, something of a shock to the little boy. The Jews who lived in the Leopoldstadt were not of the best type. A popular song in Vienna which contained the passage "When the Jews were crossing the Red Sea, all the coffee-houses in the Leopoldstadt were empty," suggests where they spent much of their time. But rents were low in this district and my father's family circumstances were poor.

Nevertheless, when my grandfather and grandmother came to see that their boy was no ordinary child, they gave him special attention; and from his schooldays, through his university days and until he became an interne in the Vienna General Hospital, he was allowed the sole use of one room, a privilege he alone enjoyed in the family.

This attention to one member of the family at the expense of other members was based, simply, on Jakob's and Amalia's firm belief that their Sigmund had been given unusual gifts, that he was destined to become famous. For him, therefore, no sacrifice was too great. He might have become spoilt and, in consequence, obnoxious to the other children; but this was not so. He showed no selfishness except on one strange point: his inflexible demand that no piano be played in the flat. He had his way then and, I might mention here, he had his way later when he had a home of his own. His attitude towards musical instruments of any kind never changed throughout his lifetime. There was never a piano in the Bergasse and not one of his children learnt to play an instrument. This was unusual in Vienna then and would probably be thought unusual today: because to be able to play the piano is considered an essential part of middle-class education. On the whole, I do not think the world has missed much through the total inability of any member of the Freud family to play "The Blue Danube": and I might add that this disability seems to have descended even to Sigmund Freud's grandchildren.

Jakob, my grandfather, had much charm, but not much luck in his business affairs in Vienna, then in the grip of a severe economic depression. Jakob became gradually helpless and ineffective in his efforts to bring up his family really well. My father would seem to have assumed some of that responsibility even when he was young. He was truly a big brother to his sisters, helping them with their lessons, explaining what was happening politically in the world of that day and supervising their choice of books. According to my Aunt Paula, he could show severity if he found them erring. He caught Paula herself spending money in a sweet shop, something she was, apparently, not supposed to do. She was admonished with so much severity that fifty years later she had neither forgiven nor forgotten it when she told the story to the small schoolboy son of the respected, and feared, big brother.

The cabinet in the humble flat in the Leopoldstadt reserved for the favourite son was not abandoned when my father went to live at the hospital in Vienna. He returned to it for week-ends and, according to my Aunt Anna, many of his friends came to see him there. The presence in the flat of five young women had not the slightest effect on these young men: the girls never received even the suspicion of a side-long glance. These young men made straight for the cabinet, disappearing without trace to begin scientific discussions with Sigmund. Aunt Anna gaily consoled herself for this neglect, certainly in later years, by admitting that while there was no scarcity of nice young ladies in Vienna ready to entertain handsome young doctors, the handsome young doctors knew there was only one Sigmund Freud in the city with whom they could discuss their problems. In any case, she recalled, the Freud girls were much too shy and diffident to make any attempt to attract attention.

It is not my purpose to tell of my father's early studies nor of his subsequent career except in so far as they affect my story. In any case, there is little I could tell at first hand, because he seldom spoke of his work to us and I have never met any of his classmates. I know that at school he often won prizes for his work, in the usual form of a book. He gave me one of these reward books when I was a boy, and this actual book, a study of animal life in the Alps by the Swiss writer, Tschudy, has assumed heirloom status. I studied it most carefully, the happy result being that when we went to the Alps, I knew much about marmots and alpine goats, and let everyone within hearing know that I knew. Eventually, I gave this book to my son, who treasures it highly; but now that his son, my grandson, is showing an interest in reading, the book given to my father as a boy may soon go to his great-grandson.

It is known how deeply my father was influenced by his work in Paris under the famous Jean Martin Charcot and how strongly this master's personality captivated him. In a sense, this influence is alive today. My father admired Charcot so much that he decided to call his eldest son after him—Jean Martin: a name quite unusual in Austria and one that now misleads the authorities in England. They often address me as "Dear Madam".

My father met my mother in April 1882 and, apparently, fell in love with her at once. They became engaged; but before they could be married they had to overcome what appeared to be an endless chain of difficulties. By a miraculous chance, the letters my father wrote to my mother during the engagement period have been preserved. None of his children had ever felt inclined to read them, holding them as much too sacred; but when Ernest Jones began his biography of my father with the approval and support of our family, it was felt that their contents might prove invaluable to him, and we entrusted them to him. He made, if I am allowed to say so, excellent use of them.

The most serious obstacle in the way of my parents' early marriage was, simply, poverty: something they endured, and enjoyed, in common; both parties were poor. My father had always preferred scientific work to ordinary medical practice; but there appeared to be no financial future in the former, and so he gave up his theoretical work and started a medical practice. As he says in his autobiography, the turning-point came in 1882 when his teacher, for whom he had the highest esteem, "corrected" Jakob's generous improvidence by advising him strongly, in view of his bad financial position, to abandon theory for practice and to enter the General Hospital in Vienna.

A few weeks before his marriage was eventually arranged in 1886, my father had to serve for a month in the Austrian army during manœuvres held at Olmuetz in Moravia. He ranked as an *Oberarzt* (full lieutenant), but he was promoted to *Regimentsarzt* (captain) during this short service. There is a letter preserved written from this place to his then best, most helpful and fatherly friend, Dr Josef Breuer, which might be quoted to show that while weapons and their ways of killing have changed dramatically since then, human attitudes to soldiering have not changed very much.

After thanking Dr Breuer for visiting his "little girl", he gives some gossip about his experience in the Austrian medical corps. He lectured on field hygiene, and the lectures had been well attended and even translated into Czech; he added gaily that he had not been confined to barracks for any crimes. "We play at war all the time," he writes; "once we even besieged a fortress. I play at being an army doctor, dealing out chits on which ghastly wounds are noted. While my battalion is attacking, I lie down on some stony field with my men. There is fake leadership and fake ammunition. Yesterday, the General rode past and called out, 'Reserves, where would you be if they had used live ammunition? Not one of you would be alive!' "

Olmuetz would seem to have had at least one attraction, a first-class café with ice, good confectionery and newspapers. But Olmuetz during the manœuvres was affected by the military system. "When two or three generals sit down together—I can't help it, but they always remind me of parakeets, for mammals don't usually dress in such colours (save for the back parts of baboons)—the whole troop of waiters surround them and nobody else would seem to exist for the waiters. Once, in despair, I grabbed a waiter by the coat-tails and shouted, 'Look here, I may be a general some time, so fetch me a glass of water!' "

That apparently worked.

My father did not admire the officer class. "An officer", he wrote, still in the letter to Dr Breuer, "is a miserable creature.

Each officer envies his equals in rank, bullies his surbordinates and fears his superiors. The higher he rises, the more he fears them." Showing how he felt himself, he adds, "I detest the idea of having inscribed on my collar how much I am worth, as if I were a sample of some product. Nevertheless, the system has gaps. The Commanding Officer, here recently from Bruenn, went into the swimming pool. I was astonished to note that his swimming trunks carried no marks of distinction." Finally, he expressed relief to know that the manœuvres would soon end. "In ten days' time I fly north and I shall forget these crazy four weeks."

My father apparently thought he had let himself go somewhat in this letter: because he ends it by apologizing for "silly tittle-tattle which has somehow slipped from my pen", before "looking forward to calling on you in Vienna for the first time with my wife."

As it turned out, it was most probably a good thing that my father abandoned a theoretical career. Several years after Bruecke had given him the advice to leave it, the small chance he had ever had of being made the head of a medical department became entirely non-existent for a man of Jewish birth, no matter how great his scientific achievements might have been. While he never said so, I think this was the chief reason that inspired him to do all in his power, and with the greatest determination, to prevent any of his sons from studying medicine.

When I was born, my father was a junior lecturer (*Privatdozent*) at the university in Vienna and practised as a specialist in nervous diseases. At that time, the family had a flat in the Suehnhaus, a palatial building facing the famous Ringstrasse on one side, and built on the site of the Ringtheatre which on the night of 8th December 1881 was burnt down during a performance of *The Tales of Hoffman* with the loss of six hundred lives.

The name given to this flat building, the Suehnhaus, which means the House of Atonement, and the fact that it was built by the Emperor Franz Josef, who gave all its revenues to the needy dependents of those who had lost their lives in the Ringtheatre fire, lends support to the story that an elderly archduchess was amongst the victims. It was said that she was being driven in her

carriage from the theatre doors across the enclosed courtyard to
the exit when, fearing that her carriage and horses might add to
the terror of the panic-stricken crowd rushing for their lives, she
ordered her coachman to stop. She, with her coachman, her
lackeys and horses lost their lives. My eldest sister, Mathilde, was
the first baby to be born in the Suehnhaus: and this was noted
by the Emperor, who sent congratulations to my parents and a
present for the baby.

I first recall my father in his medical capacity as a well-turned-
out young doctor who drove to his patients in a smart carriage
and pair called a *Fiaker*. This denoted position and wealth to an
onlooker; but, while he was regarded with great respect in
medical circles where his future as a brilliant scientist was foreseen, the truth is that my father's respectable address and the
smart carriage and pair he used hid the poverty of a man who,
with his wife, found it difficult to make both ends meet. At that
time my father was no better off than Jakob, my grandfather,
who, to use an English expression, was always on his beam ends.

An *Einspaenner*, drawn by only one horse, would have been
much cheaper; but no respectable doctor in those days would
have visited a patient in an *Einspaenner*. To use a bus or a tram
would show eccentricity, or even lunacy, which would wound
the *amour-propre* of a patient, adversely affect the remedies prescribed, and kill the reputation of a doctor.

My father as I knew him when I was a small boy was very
like any other affectionate father in Vienna, although I sometimes wonder whether or not he studied me in a psychoanalytical
light when psychoanalysis became his chief study and commanded his chief interest. It seems to me, when I come to think
of it, that I might have been a fruitful source of study because of
my first unconscious adventure not long after I was born.

It had become necessary for my mother to engage a wet-nurse.
Wet-nurses in those days were not only well paid but, for good
reasons, well fed: indeed, wet-nurses were given the most nourishing food money could buy. The woman my mother engaged,
tempted by the good pay and good food, omitted to mention that
she had no milk: and so I might have starved to death if the
trick had not been discovered in time. The story of the wicked
wet-nurse who was a dry-nurse was current in my family when

I was old enough to like stories: indeed, I never tired of hearing of the woman's expulsion in a lively cloud of indignation rising from our small household.

Like all medical men of that day, perhaps emphatically so in his case, my father gave his personal appearance much attention. He was not the slightest bit vain in the common meaning of that word. He merely submitted without objection to the deeply entrenched medical tradition that a doctor should be well turned out, and so there was never a hair out of place on his head nor on his chin. His clothing, rigidly conventional, was cut from the best materials and tailored to perfection. I can only recall one occasion during my father's long life when I saw him carelessly dressed. This happened when I was six years old.

Perhaps I had better explain that, according to my mother, the fairy godmother who gives beauty to babies was not present at my birth: she had been replaced by another fairy who gave me a beautiful imagination, and this imagination was kept alight most brightly when I was given a wonderful picture book called *Orbis Pictus*, the world in pictures. All the pictures were attractive, but none more fascinating than the pages devoted to the Bedouin, bearded men in white robes armed with long guns and jewelled daggers. Bedouin were not common in Vienna, and so I had never seen one in the flesh; but my imagination had conjured up plenty of the dream variety.

Now it happened one night when we were all asleep that a frightful explosion shook the flat building at Bergasse 19 to which we had moved four years earlier when I was two years old. Something had gone wrong with the gas supply in the flat immediately below ours, then occupied by a watchmaker. I was awake in a second to find my room brightly lighted by a glare which shone through the window; and, what was more startling, what seemed to be a live Bedouin stood at the doorway, a Bedouin with black hair standing up on end and a beard in suitable disorder. I was about to cover my head with the bedclothes in a great fright when I heard the Bedouin ask, "Are the monkeys all right?" Before the nursemaid who had rushed in with a baby in her arms could answer, the Bedouin had turned into my father in a large white bath-robe.

As it happened, the explosion created more sound, light and

fury than serious damage, although it is unlikely that the watch-maker would have survived if he had not taken the precaution of leaping through a back window to a garden. I may say that the watchmaker gave up that flat and my father took it over, using its three rooms for professional purposes and thus allowing more room for his fast-growing family.

Although my father was still a poor man when I began going to school, there was no evidence in my home that this was so. We children had all we needed, and at Christmas-time we received wonderful presents from his friends and grateful patients. We could be, and were, as naughty as any other children at times; but there was one vice of which we were never guilty, selfishness. This was not the result of admonish-ment: it simply happened in the home atmosphere created by my father and mother. It became something of a game. For instance, if we were given a box of chocolates, my mother's remark, "Teilt es euch! (divide it between you)", would result in my eldest sister Mathilde taking a sharp knife to divide a single chocolate which might not be bigger than a hazelnut into as many sections as she could manage, and distributing these to us. The game had the advantage of making a box of chocolates last a long time; but this did not affect our belief that any other method was unthinkable. I know that when I once saw a young girl at a children's party consume an entire box of chocolates at one go, I was greatly shocked and the spectacle remains as outlined in my mind as the gas explosion: also, I never spoke to that girl again.

Until the middle of last century, the inner part of Vienna was still ringed by the powerful fortifications which had helped the citizens to repel Turkish attacks. They had long become useless when Franz Josef dismantled them and gave the inner city a wide avenue which was soon adorned with handsome palaces showing a variety of architectural tastes, Greek, Gothic and Renaissance, enormously impressive to our young minds, although what charmed us most about the Ringstrasse was the trees and the well-designed parks stretching throughout nearly its whole length.

My father began work at eight every morning and it was not uncommon for him to work through until perhaps three o'clock the following morning, with breaks for luncheon and dinner, the former extended to include a walk which nearly always took in the full circle of the Ringstrasse, although sometimes he shortened it by cutting across the inner city to collect, or deliver, proofs at his publishers. However, it must not be imagined that these excursions took the form of leisurely promenades designed to enjoy the beauty of the Ringstrasse and its flowering trees in springtime. My father marched at terrific speed. The Italian bersaglieri are celebrated for the speed of their marching: when, during my travels, I saw these highly decorative soldiers tearing along, it occurred to me to think that each one of them marched like Sigmund Freud. Father might sometimes tell a favourite joke during our walks, one of a number which we had heard dozens of times without ever failing to be delighted. A certain part of Vienna, namely the Franzjosefskai, had, like all cities, its share of chimney-pots and other jutting-up adornments. My father often explained this phenomenon by telling us the story of the coffee party given by the devil's grandmother. It seems that this old lady for some reason or other was flying over Vienna with an enormous tray upon which she had put her very best coffee service, a large quantity of pots, jugs and cups and saucers of devilish design. Something happened, my father never explained just what, but I expect she entered an air pocket: at any rate the great tray turned over and the coffee service was distributed on to the roofs of Vienna, and each piece stuck. My father always enjoyed this joke as much as we did.

During his busy months, we did not see a great deal of him although, judging from his correspondence with his close friend, Dr Fliess, he saw much more of us than we then imagined, apparently contemplating our childish activities with pleasure and much amusement. During the summer holidays, which might last as long as three months, we children were in firm possession of father. He then threw aside all his professional worries and was all laughter and contentment. He had *ein froehliches Herz*, not perhaps perfectly translated as "a merry heart".

# CHAPTER III

WE were six children. The three elder children, Mathilde, myself and Oliver, were born in the Suehnhaus; the three younger, Ernst, Sophie and Anna, were born in the flat at Bergasse 19, where the family lived for forty-seven years, from 1891 to 1938. The upper part of the Bergasse adjoins a most respectable residential area, namely, the streets surrounding the Votivkirche; but the lower part, which approaches the Canal of the Danube, ends in disgrace: for here is the Tandelmarkt, somewhat like the old Caledonian Market in London, where unwanted goods accumulate and one can buy anything, from bird-cages to military decorations.

The Vienna in which we were brought up was the Imperial residence of the Emperor Franz Josef, whose personality very strongly affected the city and its people. The Emperor was not popular when he ascended the throne in the troubled year of 1848. Amalia, my grandmother, often told us children stories about the days of the revolution which she remembered vividly. It was the ordinary citizens, not the working classes, still unorganized, who opposed an absolutist régime and demanded a constitution. Although Jewish students played an important role in this struggle for freedom, it does not appear that any of my immediate ancestors were deeply involved. Amalia told us of the day when the revolutionaries came to deliver guns to the men of her family in an attempt to persuade them to take their stand at the barricades. One young man said, as he looked distastefully at a proffered gun, "How many could I shoot with this?" Apparently an estimate was given; but the young man demurred, remarking, "I am not very clever with a gun. Bring them all here, and if you do, I promise to shoot the lot in this house."

As is well-known, order was eventually restored in Austria when a constitution of sorts was granted to the people.

During the earlier years of Franz Josef's reign, a man of the people, a tailor, tried to assassinate the Emperor with a knife. He was disarmed and duly hanged on the Heath of Simmering.

Emmeline Bernays, the mother of Martha Freud

Rosa     Alexander     Anna     Adolphine     Mitzi     Paula

Sigmund Freud with his five sisters, Rosa, Anna, Adolphine, Mitzi, Paula, and his younger brother, Alexander *(from an oil painting)*

The same five sisters some sixty years later, with their mother on her 90th birthday

28c

My first snapshot of father in his study

When I was young, towards the end of last century, a not very patriotic song inspired by this incident was still sung in the quarters of the poor. It has more point in its own language, but ran something like this:

On the Heath of Simmering,
A tailor was blown away.
But it serves him right—
Why does he stitch so badly?

To commemorate the Emperor's deliverance, a Gothic-style church was built on the site of this attempt at assassination. Incidentally, the daughter-in-law of the architect, Baron Ferstel, a former patient of father's, used all the influence she could command amongst her powerful connections to make Sigmund Freud a professor despite the opposition of the Academic Senate. I shall refer again to the Ferstels in a later part of my story.

Gradually, the Emperor became popular with his people. We Freud children were all stout royalists, delighting to hear, or to see, all we could of the Imperial Court. We were always entranced to see a *Hofwagen*, a coach of the Court, and we could tell with precision the extent of the passenger's importance by the colour of the high wheels and the angle at which the magnificently liveried coachman held his whip. As I see it from this distance of time, the atmosphere of Vienna was a mixture of romance, prosperity and stiffness, mellowed, or softened, by Austrian humour.

Like the Queen in Great Britain today, the Emperor was burdened with a multitude of representative duties; but despite his reputation for stiffness, he could unbend and show some humour occasionally. My father told me a story of how Franz Josef, probably in Moravia, was visiting a small town where it became the duty of an excited and nervous mayor to present some local worthies. As each, and without doubt a great number, came forward to make his bow and to be honoured with a handshake, the mayor mentioned his name, always monotonously adding, "His Majesty, the Emperor!" "Dr Pospischil, Chief of the Hospital—His Majesty, the Emperor. Counsellor Huber, Chairman of the House and Garden Committee—His Majesty, the Emperor," and so on. After a time, Franz Josef remarked, "I think that by now, my dear Mr Mayor, the gentlemen may probably know who I am."

Nevertheless, the rules of etiquette governing Court life were extremely rigid, stronger than life perhaps and even able to threaten the law of death, it would seem. During the First World War, when Franz Josef, a very old man, was desperately ill, dying, in fact, there came a moment when he lay motionless on his bed, and his attendants, fearing that he had stopped breathing, sent hurriedly for the Emperor's personal physician.

Now it was the rule that nobody might approach His Majesty unless dressed appropriately—soldiers in parade uniform and civilians in formal evening dress. Since the summons was urgent, the doctor dared not pause to change, and thus he reached the unconscious Imperial patient in ordinary dress. While he was using his stethoscope, the Emperor opened his eyes and glanced in surprise at the doctor. "Go home!" he ordered, "and dress correctly." These, it was said in Vienna, were the Emperor's last words. The story may be false in actual fact, but its spreading about suggests the truth that Court etiquette in those days in Vienna had approached the absurd.

As I am not writing about dying Habsburgs but rather about living Freuds, I must return to my family.

My father's letters to his friend Dr Fliess show his great interest in his growing family: and perhaps this may be better evidence than I may offer as a member of the family who could be thought biased because he believes that if there is such a thing as a completely happy childhood, the children of Sigmund Freud enjoyed one. Of my eldest sister he wrote, "She is a complete little human being and, of course, thoroughly feminine." He said of me that I lived entirely in my own world of fantasy. He was much amused with the poems I composed when I was able to write, and he sent quite a number of copies to his friends. My brother Oliver, who had no time for fantasy, concerning himself only with reality as he saw it, despised my poems less for their contents and what they tried to express than for their very bad spelling. Father wrote that Oliver went on with his exact registration of routes, distances and names of places and names of mountains. The three younger children gain attention in his correspondence through their numerous afflictions. Vienna was then a very unhealthy place, and whenever an illness was going about, we managed to catch it.

In an attempt to avoid contagion and to save us from dangerous diseases, my parents did not send us to school with the other children in the district. A governess came to our flat. However, I was eventually sent to the *Volksschule*, the popular school, for my last year of elementary education. It was perhaps inevitable that the governess had not succeeded very well in preparing me for life at school with other boys who had had four years' experience. Consequently, I played a peculiar, perhaps a ridiculous, role at that school.

I loved my master; but my affection was less inspired by sentiment than by the fact that he had a large red beard which distinguished him as a recognizable person from other grown-up people. I had, as a child, much difficulty in telling one grown-up person from another: they all looked alike to me.

Since I was the first of the children to go to school, any information I could give the others about each day's experience was eagerly listened to at home and as eagerly given. Sometimes my audience included my parents. I had a villain in my daily stories, a boy who sat on the lowest bench, one who, having missed several transfers to higher classes, was older and much stronger than his class-mates. My gossip would have been very flat without this boy. I think I would have been ashamed and my audience disappointed had this villain got through a day without a misdeed. However, he never let me down.

Now it happened that when my time at this school was ending, my parents decided to withdraw me somewhat prematurely, a few weeks before the end of term, since the family were going on holiday and I was not old enough to be left. On that last day at school, and as soon as the master entered, I got up and marched to the platform upon which his desk stood and, having mounted this, I bowed and made him a little speech. I thanked him for all he had done for me and ended by saying how sorry I was to leave. The whole class was startled into silence; indeed it was flabbergasted to a boy, because such improvised oratory had never been heard in that school before; but the teacher, with rare sensibility, appreciated the simplicity of my intention and was moved to say, "Freud, I wish you will always remain as you are now."

Now I know exactly what he meant by those few words, as will some of my readers: because they, certainly some of those who are my age, may easily recall words of a very different kind spoken by a teacher, biting cruel words which, unforeseen by the one who has used them, re-echo throughout a lifetime and go on hurting. But at that time the red-bearded master's words startled me. I knew he had not met a witch at the school door, a witch who had given him the right to make one wish; but, superstitious as I then was (and still am), I feared that a wish made by a schoolmaster one loved might have the quality of a spell. And while it is true that I did not, of course, remain a child in literal obedience to the teacher's wish, it took me an awfully long time to grow up. I know that in the lower classes of the Gymnasium I was found to be not mentally ripe for the tasks set; and my very slow progress must have caused my father great anxiety. Fortunately the good teacher's spell did not last for ever.

From what I have said it will show that the education of Sigmund Freud's children was different from that of other children. I may not say it was better; it was simply of a different pattern. I know that we Freud children did things and said things that other people found strange. Some, like my teacher with the red beard, found them moving. I expect our upbringing might be called "liberal", if one may use that much abused word. We were never ordered to do this, or not to do that; we were never told not to ask questions. Replies and explanations to all sensible questions were always given by our parents, who treated us as individuals, persons in our own right. I would not presume to advocate this kind of bringing up: it was how Sigmund Freud's children were brought up.

But there was no lack of discipline. My mother ruled her household with great kindness and with an equally great firmness. She believed in punctuality in all things, something then unknown in leisurely Vienna. There was never any waiting for meals: at the stroke of one everybody in the household was seated at the long dining-room table and at the same moment one door opened to let the maid enter with the soup while another door opened to allow my father to walk in from his study to take his place at the head of the table facing my mother at the other end. We had as long as I can remember a *Herrschaftskoechin*, a cook who did no work outside her kitchen; there was a housemaid who waited at table and also received father's patients. There was the governess for the elder children and a nanny for the younger, while a charwoman came each day to do the rough work.

My mother knew how to manage servants. They loved and respected her and gave of their best. It is true that she kept the same servants for years on end: and even in those days this was most exceptional in Vienna.

The meal at one o'clock, the *Mittagessen*, was the principal meal of the day in our home. There was always soup, meat and vegetables, and a sweet: the usual three-course midday dinner, varied during appropriate seasons when, in springtime, we had an additional course in the way of asparagus. Later, in the summer, we might have corn on the cob, or Italian artichokes. My father was not fussy over food but, like most people, he had his likes and dislikes. He was particularly fond of Italian artichokes; but he never touched cauliflower and he was not fond of chicken. "One should not kill chickens," he sometimes said; "let them stay alive and lay eggs."

My father's favourite dish was *Rindfleisch*, boiled beef as it is called in England; and we had this three or four times a week but never with the same sauce. Our *Herrschaftskoechin* could produce at least seven different kinds and all of them delicious. One may have boiled beef in England; but I cannot imagine myself eating it without a distaste produced, perhaps, by an odious comparison with what my mother served. She must have shared a Viennese secret, how to make the *Rindfleisch* so juicy and tasty. The *Mehlspeise*, the sweet, was always a work of supreme culinary art. *Apfelstrudel* has since been introduced in England; but it is still not the same.

It would be ungrateful and ungracious if I praised the country of my birth, Austria, which expelled me, and criticized harshly a country that has received me and given me hospitality; and this I will never do except when I compare the cooking of both countries: Austrian cooking is definitely much better than English cooking.

Despite the excellent and very nourishing food our mother

served so lavishly, we all remained quite slim. I recall that we had no patience for stout people,whom we despised and ridiculed. I might remark that I, myself, had no objection to eating cauliflower; but my father's dislike produced a certain loyalty which allowed me to affect a repugnance equally strong. But this loyalty was not strong enough to take in chicken, which I loved and ate as much as I could when there were guests for dinner and my mother served chicken for their sakes.

While we children were at home, my mother was kept busy from morning until night, and I cannot remember her enjoying a quiet moment to sit down and to relax with a good book: and she loved to read a good book. My parents had many friends, most of them Jewish and members of the upper middle classes, and thus few afternoons passed without the appearance of at least one visitor and often more. While my mother was entertaining guests we children would be left in the charge of the reigning governess or perhaps the nanny.

My parents always insisted that their children should have plenty of fresh air and as much exercise as possible; and since the back garden of the house where we lived was a small and pitiful affair, we were always taken out daily to one of the many public parks. Since the parks most popular with our governess or the nanny were all on the Ringstrasse, on that circuit around which my father used to storm his way, the small detachment of his offspring followed his tracks but at a much slower pace and with less determination. I recall chiefly the nanny called Josefine who looked after my youngest sister, and, after all these years, I can still recall clearly our little procession—the baby lying in the pram and the taller children walking at its side, sometimes with their hands on its rails. There were, of course, no motor-cars and the crossings were much safer then than they must be now. But other dangers lurked.

Our promenades took us past the university and the parliament building, and both were storm-centres in those days of political unrest. That *mélange* of disunited nations forming the Austro-Hungarian Empire tried to make democracy work, but with scant success. Whenever there was a deadlock in parliament, the Emperor had the constitutional right to dissolve parliament and to govern the Empire himself. When this happened there were turbulent demonstrations which were regarded by the Government, in effect the Emperor, with varying degrees of patience. If the Emperor lost his patience, he used the armed forces.

On one of these latter occasions our little detachment, commanded by Josefine, found itself between the rioters and some charging dragoons. It narrowly escaped being trampled down, perambulator and all, under the hooves of the cavalry. The incident was, of course, highly alarming; but in no way did it affect my personal admiration for the mounted forces.

We occasionally saw outbreaks of violence near the university and I little thought then that, many years later, I myself would be a combatant, to be wounded but, fortunately, not arrested. One day we saw uniformed police, as always in pairs, leading between them somewhat dishevelled young students.

Josefine ordered us not to look, giving it as her firm opinion that anybody arrested by the police must be a wicked criminal at whom a really good child should not look. My mother, who was with us that day, promptly intervened by contradicting Josefine, explaining that a man arrested in political strife could very well be a brave man and, possibly, a noble character. He could be struggling for ideas, or risking his life and liberty for convictions which he believed to be right.

I recall both opinions with much bias towards that of my mother; but when years later I had learnt to think and to consider political movements, I found myself wondering why my mother, who could hardly have been more conservative or more law-abiding, could show sympathy for rebels against constituted authority. I am sure now that her attitude on the Ringstrasse that day of the students' riot was a direct result of her deep love for my father who, at heart, had always been a rebel against convention.

Still, that nanny, Josefine, had great influence over me. More than sixty years have passed since those carefree Vienna days; but I never pass a canteen, or see a picture of a canteen at some great factory where the workers gather for meals, without recalling the Mensa Academica, near the university buildings, under the arcades, where students could get cheap meals. Josefine never failed to explain as we passed that only very poor people, people destitute and without decent pride, would eat in such a place.

Canteens, of course, have important uses in modern life; but I have yet to recover from that impression indelibly fixed in my mind.

My father described his own nurse as an old and ugly woman, a Catholic, who used to take him to her church services in Freiberg, possibly with the idea of laying early foundations of a conversion. I do not think for one moment that Josefine had any thoughts of this kind, but one day when I was out with her alone, the other children being left at home for some reason I have forgotten, she took me into the nearby Votivkirche to a service. The church was crowded; the ceremonial was magnificent and colourful, and I was greatly impressed by the preacher: but I suspect Josefine's object was merely to sit down, not to impress a little Jewish boy with the splendour and dignity of a Catholic service. Possibly she needed spiritual food, and as she could not, or dared not, dump me anywhere, she towed me in behind her.

It is only, I think, ungracious children who will pick faults in the way their parents have brought them up, especially when they have been given only the deepest love and understanding; but events, not foreseen when I was a child, do allow me to criticize the lessons we were given in English.

Our English teacher's qualifications for her work were not impressive, or so they seem in retrospect. She was the sister of our governess, who recommended her. She had never been in England, and it is more than likely that she had never heard an English person speak. However, the recommendation was accepted by my parents and we were given "English" lessons for quite a time.

This English we were taught had doubtless an origin in England, but it had come a very long way through generations of Austrians until it had lost any serious resemblance to what is spoken in the United Kingdom. It had gained an idiom of its own and was spoken and understood in the British internment camps established in 1940 when the usually trusting British people naturally showed suspicion of all Teutonic peoples in their midst. Later it was used successfully in the Pioneer Corps when calmer councils prevailed; but while we Austrian exiles thought it a pleasant, even a beautiful, language, those British clever enough to understand a few of its words thought rather differently.

My father, of course, most certainly did not realize the disadvantages we might suffer later in learning this quaint Austrian-English; and I think this was because he had not the slightest ear for music.

As a matter of fact, he had a supreme sense of language himself and could speak fluently any language he had studied. As far as I could judge, his accent was good. He spoke English, French, Italian, and, as our mother often told us with great pride, Spanish. I never had a chance to hear him speak Spanish, but as far as I know he corresponded in their own language with Spanish editors who translated his collected papers. He mastered Latin and Greek at his Gymnasium.

It happened one day that a very close friend of my father, one whose life was devoted to the study of the Ancients and their world, came to call at the Bergasse. I was alone with my parents and their guest after dinner when we were drinking coffee; and when the conversation turned to education in classical literature, I was encouraged to recite the opening verses of Homer's *Iliad* in Greek. I began with enthusiasm, but after a few lines I lost the place in my memory and felt I should start all over again. Detecting this thought, my father instantly began where I had halted and marched along very well, certainly with more assurance than I had shown, although I had, in fact, learnt the lines only a few weeks earlier and my father had not recited them for thirty years. However, he, too, reached a point where his memory failed and he began hesitating, perhaps showing a little inaccuracy. Instantly, the guest took over and, being a professional one might say, easily excelled the two amateurs.

Indeed, he excelled so magnificently that he seemed to forget his hosts and began reciting endlessly, it seemed, from the *Iliad*; becoming more inspired every minute, and shouting louder and louder until, carried away by the beauty of the ancient poem, he showed signs of deep emotion. When a tear trickled down his beard, father threw me a quick glance with the slightest indication of a smile. Father had the rare ability of being able to send a message with a small gesture, the kind of message which would demand a sentence, or even a paragraph from another. He knew that emotion of this kind in an adult could produce an hysterical giggle from an adolescent boy, and he was warning me that, as a good boy, I should wait patiently until our guest came down to earth again quietly, not with a jerk, which might happen if I ridiculed him by laughing. My mother, who knew no Greek and, in consequence, was without any admiration for Homer's immortal epic, had quietly withdrawn earlier.

My mother shared my father's ability to control his emotions. When the nursery rooms my brother and I had slept in became two adjoining studies with maps, little desks and the usual bookshelves, a gymnastic contrivance, a trapeze, was hung on the doorway between the two rooms. My mother was sitting in one of the rooms when we were practising, swinging head-down from the trapeze above the necessary mattress on the floor below us. When my turn came, I lost my grip and fell, not alas fairly on to the mattress but against a piece of furniture. My forehead was cut somewhat seriously and from this incision, several inches long, blood began flowing alarmingly. My mother, who had been quietly sewing, did not drop her work. She merely paused long enough to ask the governess to telephone to the doctor who lived a few doors away from our home and to tell him to call immediately.

I was impressed by the amount of blood, but I scrambled to my feet without help, quite surprised that the accident had produced no excitement whatever, not the suspicion of panic, not even one outcry of horror. A few minutes later the doctor, a great big man with a massive black beard, had stitched the wound and adorned me with an impressive white bandage.

I mentioned a telephone; and it is true that in those middle nineties we had one; but telephones were still rarities in Vienna although doctors were the first people to have them. Ours was installed when I was six years old and the noisy contraption was looked on by us children with awe and curiosity. It was fixed fairly high up on the wall of the landing and, apart from the fact that we could not reach it without help, it was a long time before we dared to use it. In any case there was no one to whom we might telephone; none of our friends had telephones then.

My father hated the telephone and avoided its use whenever possible. As everything in our home was arranged to harmonize with his wishes, all precautions were taken to save him from using it. I raised this point with my brother and my two sisters who now live in London, asking them two questions. I asked them if they knew why father detested the telephone. They said they did not know. I then asked if they had ever spoken to father on the telephone, and two of them replied, "Never!" One sister admitted that she did speak to father once when she called up our home. He answered because there was no one else at home. I spoke to my father only once on the telephone and that was during the First World War when I was passing through Vienna without being able to see him. He had not seen me for some time and he wanted to talk to me and, for once, he overcame his prejudice. His voice reached me with clarity and apparently he did not miss a word I said.

My own theory is that when my father communicated by speech with another human being, the conversation had to be a very personal thing. He looked one straight in the eye, and he could read one's thoughts. Then it was an absolute impossibility to attempt to say anything that was not precise truth: not that I had ever any occasion to try to tell him anything but the truth. Father, aware of this power when looking at a person, felt he had lost it when looking at a dead telephone mouthpiece.

My father left the education of his children almost entirely in the hands of our mother, but this did not affect his deep interest as he stood by and smilingly observed. And always, when something happened to us, some unhappy incident or accident which assumed the proportions of a tragedy in our young minds, when, in fact, we needed him, he always came down from his Olympian heights to help rescue us. We were good children, although I, a good enough average kind of boy, was, in my mother's judgement, the black sheep of the little flock. And it is true that I got into trouble more often than my brothers and sisters. However, this had an important advantage in that I was more often rescued by father.

I recall one occasion when my five brothers and sisters caught a variety of contagious maladies, everything available at the time except smallpox and plague. One of the affected children wrote a letter to a friend which said, "Oliver has German measles, Ernst has whooping-cough and Sophie has mumps. All send regards." The joke, instantly detected by the others—maladies appearing to send greetings—is more apparent in my native language than in English.

There was I, fit and well, in what amounted to a children's hospital with a good chance of catching one or all of the prevalent maladies. The prospect was perhaps more interesting than alarming; but it was one of the occasions when my father came to the rescue. Taking me by the hand he led me to the house of a friend, a widow with one son a few years older than myself who was studying the piano and promising himself to be a concert pianist of the highest repute. Incidentally this boy kept the promise; he did become a famous pianist and travelled the world. He miraculously escaped death in a great Japanese earthquake, only to lose his life a little later in a car accident in Italy.

But I was not to anticipate this glory when I found myself lonely and unhappy away from my parents, my sisters and my brothers. That boy and I began a series of fights almost at once; and because he had developed some muscles and my arms were still as thin as sticks, I always lost. The day I left I attempted revenge for all these defeats. I handed the young gentleman a small sketch showing a donkey with very long ears bending over a piano. The best translation I can make in English of the legend written on my sketch in verse form is:

> Here is your picture, friend, I say—
> An ass enjoys a piano to play.

This correspondence was sent to my father; but instead of reprimanding me for inflicting an act of gross ingratitude on the widow who adored her son, he showed himself to be amused.

The climate of Vienna allows open-air skating for up to three months in the winter, when the temperature seldom rises above freezing-point; and after school hours we used to skate on a natural ice rink in the famous Augarten. Three of us were there one day, Mathilde, Ernst and myself. Ernst and I had crossed hands and were enjoying ourselves sailing in wide circles over the ice when, as can so easily happen to a couple skating, we collided with an elderly gentleman with a long white beard. While we did not knock him over, we unhappily succeeded in throwing him off his not-too-secure balance and he went staggering about in a confusion which was very funny indeed. The high spirits of Ernst allowed him to laugh and to make some not very kind remarks which the old gentleman overheard. These compared him with an old billy-goat and, very naturally, he became angry, shouting and gesticulating enough to attract the attention of other skaters, including a highly skilled figure-skater who, thinking I was the culprit, and being a tracted by the role of a defender of venerable age, swooped past me, pausing somewhat in his flight to slap my face: the face, he imagined, of some insolent young hooligan.

Normally, a slap on the face in those days would not mean much to a boy: it would be accepted as part of his education; but, as it happened, that slap on the face was a tragedy to me. In some strange way, or for some queer reason, I had developed what today might be called a complex about "honour". Attached to me in some way was this immaterial element, or whatever you might call it, known to army officers and students of duelling societies as their honour: something which might not be assaulted except at the assaulter's peril.

I tried to throw myself at my assailant, a grown-up man who was not, however, bigger than myself; but I was held back by a crowd of onlookers who had followed us to the outer edge of the rink where, still wearing skates, all stood uneasily on the wooden boarding and all expressed themselves loudly and at the same time. The incident had created a sensation. The figure-skater kept at a safe distance; but the man in charge of the rink, being armed with authority, was much less nervous. He confiscated my season-ticket. The assault, and now this act of expulsion, would have trampled my precious honour into the earth if the ground had not been frozen so hard.

While the contestants faced each other on the wooden boarding, arguing angrily, a slight diversion was created by a small fat man who was trying to reach us by climbing up the frozen slope from the rink leading to the boarding. He fell and slipped a number of times; but at last he reached us with his hands and face scratched and his black clothes very much soiled. After some difficulty, he succeeded in fighting his way through the crowd and reached me. He gave me his card and introduced himself as a lawyer. He said he had been a witness of the assault, that he would conduct a case against the aggressor himself and that, in consequence, I had the best chance of winning the case.

This offer only added to my feeling of desperation. In all the codes of honour I had studied with so much care, it was always insisted that under no circumstances could an aggrieved party carry his grievance to a law court: such an act, it was said, was to sink into an abyss of shame and cowardice. To make matters worse, I already knew something of what happened in such cases when, in Vienna of that day, there were fixed charges for petty offences. The fine inflicted for a slap on the face was about half a crown in English money, but there would probably be some reduction when the slapped face belonged to a boy.

The lawyer, not, of course, a representative of the Viennese legal profession, evidently thought we were the children of a wealthy family and that his defence of me might be profitable in different ways. He was given an angry refusal, and withdrew somewhat crestfallen. The incident was tending to fade out in a miserable anticlimax when my sister Mathilde took a hand.

Mathilde, an attractive and lively girl, was very popular and never lacked plenty of cavaliers on the ice. She marshalled as many of these as she could and led an expedition to the care-taker's office. He, a big and red-faced man, was helpless before this attack and, doubtless, fearing he might get into trouble, bowed before the storm and gave Mathilde my season-ticket. I, still concerned with my wounded honour, had no idea what my sister and her friends had done to the big red-faced man; but I know that when he came out of the office he seemed much smaller and the colour had left his cheeks. Mathilde returned to me at the head of her troop, waving the season-ticket victoriously like a banner of victory.

We returned home with our story, all talking at once to our parents, to whom the smallest of our adventures was interesting and worth their attention; and I think I might have enjoyed it as much as Mathilde and Ernst if my face had not been slapped by an expert skater and my honour grievously assaulted and left wounded and bleeding metaphorically. My whole future, it seemed to me, had been destroyed by this disgrace. Clearly, when my time for military service came, I could never be an officer. I might be a potato-peeler; I might be the man who whitewashed the stones on the parade ground; my military service could be spent emptying garbage pails or cleansing latrines: but clearly

I could never be a proud officer. I was dishonoured; I was an outcast. Life, I felt, was no longer worth living. After all these years, it all seems so utterly ridiculous; then the pain was real.

Father had listened to our story with deep interest, but when all the details of the adventure had been exhausted, he asked me to go with him into his study. He told me to sit down and to tell him the whole story from beginning to end, much as I am telling it now. He listened intently as I told him everything, convincing him, it seemed, that my honour, then so precious to me, had indeed been assaulted and that the very serious view I took of the incident was perfectly natural.

I have a good memory for details, but I can recall very little of what he said; but I do know that after a very few minutes what had seemed a soul-destroying tragedy assumed normal proportions: it became only an unpleasant and meaningless trifle.

Had father used hypnosis or psychoanalysis on me? I really do not know.

Once, in the Bavarian Alps, I watched a gamekeeper releasing a small animal caught in a poacher's net. Very tenderly, one after the other, he began removing the cords that held the little beast, showing no hurry and resisting the animal's struggles without impatience until all were thrown aside and it was free to run away and forget all about it.

I had been caught in a net of hurt pride, prejudice, fear and humiliation: my father saw that I could not find my way to freedom alone. I expect he removed each cord that held me with the same patience and determination shown by the Bavarian game-keeper. He loosened from my disturbed mind all the fetters of fear and humiliation and set me free. As I said above, I can recall little or nothing of what he said to me, and I think this is typical of all similar treatment when a trauma is successfully dealt with: one forgets not only the injury but also the cure. However, I do remember that father did not deny the moral right to hit back when one is hit.

## CHAPTER IV

As I have already explained, we children saw little of our father when, for much of the year, he worked for anything from sixteen to eighteen hours a day. That, of course, can be the fate of many children of medical men concerned with ills, mental and physical, which attack human beings without reference to the clock; but, while this did not apply to us, it seemed to us that we saw nothing at all of him because of the contrast his presence produced in our summer holidays. Then it was not often that he allowed himself to be away from us from early morning until we were put to bed.

During my earlier years, father's income from his practice fluctuated a good deal; there were periods when particular economy in running his home was absolutely essential. If such a period happened during the summer, we travelled third class to whatever holiday resort my parents had chosen. This was a challenge to my mother which I think she enjoyed meeting. Uncle Alexander had some influence with the railway people, certainly to the extent of getting a whole third-class compartment reserved for us. In Austria in those days a third-class compartment could only offer hard wooden benches; but mother, with the help of rugs, cushions and pillows, soon turned the shabby place into luxurious sleeping-quarters with quite a home atmosphere, which did not, however, destroy our feelings of enjoying an adventure. She always calculated precisely how many children could be fitted comfortably along the seats and, if there were surplus children, a hammock or two might be slung. She and the nurse, if any, huddled themselves in corners. My father would have joined us willingly, but what was a victorious battle to my mother would have been, she knew, an ordeal to him: and she always arranged, possibly by subtle means unknown to us, to make him travel alone and in comfort.

When I was old enough to think of such things, I admired the way my mother managed to direct and to keep in perfect order our summer expeditions. There were children, occasionally one or

An early family group showing my parents with five of their six children and mother's sister, Aunt Minna

The three brothers, Ernst, Oliver and Martin, rowing on the
Thumsee, a small lake in Bavaria

The villa in Berchtesgaden, where Sigmund Freud wrote the
*Interpretation of Dreams*

two servants and always much baggage. The servants, perhaps a governess and a nurse, quite efficient in familiar home surroundings, seemed to break down and to become both helpless and useless from the moment the expedition began, and everything was left to mother,who, during one of these advances from the home base, was expecting an addition to the family. But she was never perturbed, and she never overlooked a detail, exchanging her normal role of an ordinary, practical housewife for the cold and calculating organizing genius of a senior officer of the Prussian General Staff.

I do not know how the governess and nurse felt during these journeys; mother's efficiency may have frozen them into at least jelly; but we children loved the trains, the fuss and the movement, anticipating the start for weeks. Someone, I cannot recall who it was, gave each of us a travelling-satchel which could be slung over one's shoulders with a strap; and days before the journey began, these satchels were packed and unpacked and carried about with us.

"Can one already *see* the journey?" my impatient sister Sophie asked father during one of these delightful periods of anticipation; and this question assumed the status of a classic in our family. My father used it many, many years later in a letter to my brother Ernst a few days before he left on his last long journey from Vienna to London.

The earliest holiday I can remember clearly was one made to the Adriatic in the autumn of 1895, a few months before my youngest sister, Anna, was born.

Vienna is far from the sea. The Adriatic, although a long train journey from the capital, including a night, offered the nearest salt water. In those days much of the Adriatic coast was part of the Austrian Empire. Now, of course, that part belongs to Yugoslavia and names have changed. We went to Lovrana, now called Lovran, a small and quiet fishing village near the much more fashionable health resort of Abazzia, in turn called Opatija. The hotel we stayed at was the only one in the village; and I recall it as being most comfortable. The weather, as is usual in this part of Europe in early autumn, was glorious.

The coast is rocky but in front of the hotel there was a

small cove which may have been excavated or may have been natural, and this had a narrow strip of white sand which met clear, shallow water where children could safely splash about. We spent every minute we could of every day in this little cove, always protesting when taken away for supper and bed.

Uncle Alexander, still a bachelor, was with us, and he and father were seldom out of the water, becoming completely sunburnt so far as the decorous bathing-costumes of the last century would permit. These costumes covered men's shoulders and even parts of their arms. Ladies of that era were even worse off: they had to cover their legs with long black stockings. I cannot recall ever having seen my mother or her sister in bathing-costumes, either on the Adriatic coast or at holiday places where there were lakes. It is probable that both were much too modest, or vain, to show themselves even in nineteenth-century bathing-costumes; possibly they could not swim.

Father and Uncle Alexander naturally went farther out from the shore than we children were permitted to go and when, as sometimes happened, they refused to come ashore even for lunch, so much did they enjoy every minute in that warm salt water, a waiter would wade or swim out to them balancing a tray with refreshments and even cigars and matches.

This Adriatic coast has the inevitable beauty of any rocky headlands that meet a sea free of mud-flats; in many respects it resembles the coast of Cornwall in England, but the Adriatic coast, blessed with a sub-tropical climate, can be adorned with palms and lush vegetation. There are no green fields and hedgerows as in Cornwall, but the atmosphere is much softer and more congenial to those who would play, those who would sit and think, and to those who would merely sit. I have visited the Adriatic many times since that first visit under the command of my mother.

Over the porch of our hotel were vines and fig-trees, and it was possible for my sister Mathilde, the tallest of the children, to climb from a chair to a table and bite off the figs which were ripe then. When we could drag ourselves away from the water we made many excursions along leafy lanes to neighbouring villages and one day we enjoyed a great adventure. My younger brother Oliver, then an unusually pretty boy with big black eyes, went too near a cage where a monkey lived and was scratched and bitten. This threw the local fishwives into a great state of melodramatic Italian excitement as they began crying and gesticulating, a performance which I think would have been less like a scene from *Cavalleria Rusticana* if I, or some other ugly little boy, had been bitten. These haggard old women showed much sympathy and did all they could to help Oliver recover from his accident: attention which, like all handsome people, he accepted as his due in those days. Oliver always inspired admiration from strangers we met, when his brothers could hardly attract a glance.

It was not for fifteen years that the Freud family again enjoyed a holiday at the seaside. My father had been happy at Lovrana; but he much preferred mountains to the sea; and so, year after year, with two exceptions, to the mountains we went—to Styria, Bavaria and the Tyrol. Most places were visited more than once. Although there was no change in our way of life at the Bergasse, no more being spent on food, clothing, service and entertainments, when father's financial position gradually improved, the difference was marked during holidays: we went farther afield, travelled more comfortably and stayed at more expensive hotels.

My father always expresse⁻ᵈ extreme dislike of Vienna, so that when for a number of reasons it was decided that the family should spend the best part of the summer of 1900 at Schloss Bellevue, a mansion on the hills four or five miles from the Bergasse, he wrote to his friend, Dr Fliess: "I am as hungry as a young man for the spring, and sun, and flowers and a stretch of blue water. I hate Vienna with a positively personal hatred and, just the contrary of the giant Antaeus, I draw fresh strength whenever I remove my feet from the soil of this city which is my home. For the children's sake I shall have to renounce distance and mountains, and enjoy the constant view of Vienna from Bellevue. . . ."

But, evidently, life at Schloss Bellevue turned out better than he had expected. On 12th June he wrote again to the same friend: "Life at Bellevue is turning out very pleasantly for every one.

The mornings and evenings are delightful. The scent of acacia
and jasmine has followed the lilac and laburnum; the wild roses
are in bloom and everything, as even I notice, seems to have suddenly burst forth."

I am not convinced that Sigmund Freud's often-expressed dislike of Vienna was either deep-seated or real. It is not difficult
for a London man, or a New York man, both devoted to their
respective home cities, to say, "How I hate London; how I loathe
New York." They are speaking the truth of a day, of an hour or
of a moment: not necessarily a fixed attitude. And my own feeling is that sometimes my father hated Vienna, and that sometimes
he loved the old city, and that, in a general sense, he was devoted.
He could have left Vienna at any time during the many secure
years before the Hitler shadow began dimming the city's gay
sky; but he never did, nor did he, so far as I know, ever seriously
contemplate emigrating. And even at the end, when every consideration compelled him to leave, he left with great reluctance
and only after strong persuasion.

Father was not a bit unsocial: he liked company and it was
usual to see him at summer resorts in animated conversation
walking up and down with newly won friends. These were educated people, not highbrow—leading men in commerce or industry and perhaps an odd newspaper editor, an artist or
politician. But Schloss Bellevue was rather different, because you
had here people of the *petite bourgeoisie*; and although class
distinctions as such could not interest Sigmund Freud, it was a
simple fact that they spoke, in effect, a different language. He
had moved with ease in the Paris *salon* of the world-famous Jean
Martin Charcot; but he tended to feel utterly lost and at a
loose end with the people who had taken rooms or apartments
at Bellevue. They had no common ground for any sort of conversation.

There was an elderly father with four or five sons, all footballers and all good-natured. They would be called "hearties" in
England. These young men treated me very well indeed, letting
me often join in their football games; and I remain especially
grateful to the eldest son, who showed me how to treat the care-
taker's children who were about my own age and tended to
bully me, something I might otherwise have accepted meekly

because of my rather sheltered upbringing. He showed me how to defend myself against this aggression. Nor was my father entirely unaffected by the friendliness of the footballers, who, it must be admitted, treated him with due respect even when, on one occasion, they asked him to join them in a game of skittles. The mansion had a large covered-in skittle-alley. Father hesitated and said, "Oh—no, no!" but mother, in a holiday spirit, persuaded him to agree. Everybody took off his coat and the game began.

Father had naturally a good aim and the balls thrown by him rolled powerfully along the alley, causing respectable havoc amongst the skittles. Watching him, I blushed somewhat, or I suppose I did, when he followed what seemed to me an old-fashioned habit of running a few yards after the ball when it had left his hand. I thought this looked odd and I was in something of a panic, fearing the footballers might laugh and ridicule him; but nobody laughed and the game went on, father doing very well and very nearly winning. He was, in fact, beaten by one of the young men who played rather better.

This young man assumed a mock triumph and stepping to the door struck an attitude, spreading out his arms as he exclaimed: "Hear me, one and all. I am the victor. Now Europe may kiss my hand."

Father did not enjoy this. He excused himself politely and, offering his arm to mother, took her for an evening walk.

Unfortunately, the Freud relations with the footballer family deteriorated soon after this incident. The young man who had beaten father at skittles, who was quite a lad, returned one evening to Bellevue in a *Fiaker* with a young woman of doubtful gaiety and indifferent manners. Worse still, he was so very drunk that his brothers had to carry him from the carriage into the house. What happened to the young woman of gay but dubious appearance remains unknown to me; she was lost sight of during the fuss that ensued when the footballer's father saw the young man's condition, which, he felt, required immediate medical attention. This was given obligingly by my father, who did all that was necessary, but when, shortly after this incident, another of the brothers returned home seriously ill with the same complaint in the middle of the night and Doctor Freud was called from his bed, Doctor Freud became angry and forbade them, once and for all, to disturb him again. After this incident all diplomatic relations between the Freuds and the footballers at Schloss Bellevue were terminated.

# CHAPTER V

THE selection of a family summer holiday resort was always father's duty, and he took this very seriously indeed: it became, in fact, a fine art in later years when he acted as a kind of pioneer, ranging about the mountains until he found what he believed would be popular with the family.

Until 1895, while we were still growing, our summer plans were not ambitious: our parents were content with places not more than a two- or three-hour railway journey from Vienna, like those at the foot of the Rax and the Schneeberg, easterly spurs of the alpine chain. But after 1895, we went farther afield, to the Alt-Aussee, which was not, however, an unusual nor adventurous choice, because many of Vienna's middle-class families, a good proportion of whom were Jewish, went there. Alt-Aussee was not then a popular tourist resort with hotels designed chiefly for tourists, although there were a few old-established inns.

Most people rented cottages for the summer months from the local inhabitants: small farmers, cattle-breeders and salt-mine employees. Relations between temporary landlords and summer tenants were friendly and even cordial, and this applied to our family although we went to Aussee not more than three consecutive summers. Some families had been going to Aussee all their lives, becoming so intimately related to their landlords that it was quite common to find local peasant children spending Christmas in Vienna with their parents' summer tenants.

The house we rented stood on a hill with a magnificent view of the mountains, always a serene joy to those who really love mountains, profoundly true of our family and father in particular: a feeling he gave me, a priceless gift I still treasure. And within a stone's throw began pine forests stretching, it seemed to us, to the end of the world, over hills and mountains for ever and for ever. These forests were our summer playgrounds.

The high land upon which our cottage stood was called the Obertressen, and it lay half-way between the market town of Markt-Aussee and the lake nestling amidst forests and mountains of impressive beauty. Although the waters of the lake were dark-green they yet had the quality of almost transparent clarity.

It was all very lovely, this country; but, it must be admitted, some of its loveliness was the direct result of an extremely wet climate, even wetter than the English Lake District to which it bears resemblance. Most of the lush meadows were somewhat marshy, a condition that allowed certain flowers to bloom in abundance, particularly narcissi, which grew wild and whitened the meadows in late spring. Father found great delight in the remarkable variety of edible fungi that grew in the forests and clearings.

The dominating feature of the landscape was the Dachstein, the highest mountain in the district, rising to over 9,000 feet with a snow-covered crest, the source of a glacier. The Dachstein, which could always be seen from our windows and balconies in clear weather, exerted a great fascination over me when I was a child, a fascination that never faded even when, in much later years, I crossed it a number of times and climbed not only to its summit but also to several of the less accessible peaks rising from the glacier. I cannot resist telling of an adventure I had years later when, with a friend and his brother, I set out from Aussee to climb one of the Dachstein lesser peaks, a bleak icy rock rising from the glacier. The adventure was of that kind which one enjoys so much more after it is over than when it is in hazardous operation. Father always listened most attentively when told of my mountaineering attempts, and he was easily amused if anything strange or unusual occurred, particularly so if it bordered on the ridiculous.

This peak was not often attempted and, in consequence, there was no marked pathway leading to its base nor had any attempt been made to supply any kind of aids. Equipped with rope, ice-axe and crampons, I acted as guide on the short but very steep part of the ascent where one had to hack out steps in the ice. There was, in fact, only one dangerous and exposed stretch where the ascent crossed a steep and narrow ravine under the summit. I, followed by my friend,who, with his brother, was secured by my rope, had got across the ravine quite safely and, aware that the ravine was badly exposed to falling stones and ice, I urged the brother to make haste to get it over. "Hurry on!" I shouted.

My order had no effect. Leaning on his stick and fumbling under the tight rope to reach his pocket, I saw him digging out something from his pocket which turned out to be a sandwich; and this he began calmly eating. I shouted at him, asking him if he had gone completely mad; but my friend, apologizing, explained that his brother was subject to sudden and severe pangs of hunger during which he simply had to eat a *Schinkensemmel*, a ham sandwich. Nothing could be done. In very real danger shared by the three of us, I had to wait until the snack was eaten.

I might remark here that since that adventure I have taken many beginners up mountains, but nearly always they have been girls. Girls are less stubborn and more obedient.

It was when I told father of the *Schinkensemmel* incident that I learnt for the first time that he had crossed the Dachstein from the south side, going alone. This was most probably in 1891 when he visited Schladming for a week-end. It was an exploit of which he could well have been proud, but he had never mentioned it. He had had no previous alpine training. On the north side there is a long and safe bridle-path leading to the Dachstein summit in a series of endless serpentines; but the southerly route that father took is usually attempted only by experienced climbers, or at least with a guide. The way leads over a wall of steep rocks. There are iron foot-rests, ladders and steel ropes to make the ascent less difficult in good weather, but when these are covered with ice and snow, they become a hindrance rather than a help to a climber. To climb the Dachstein from the south side, one had to have great powers of perseverence, to be free of vertigo, and to be strong and steady with hand and foot. In a word, that ascent over rocks and ice demanded courage of a high order.

Father told me that he had found not the slightest difficulty in making this expedition nor was he conscious of any danger or discomfort. However, the ease with which he did what he wanted to do in climbing in his younger days never affected his sympathy and understanding when I told him of my own alpine exploits in later years.

But I have climbed ahead of my story and I must retrace my steps back to the years between 1896 and 1898—sixty years ago, a long time it will seem to younger people who, in time, will learn that events of their childhood remain more sharply outlined than much, even of greater significance, that has occurred in their middle years.

When we arrived at the cottage at Aussee, we were always greeted with a charming and useful present by our landlords. This was a small model of a trough cleverly designed in fresh farm butter and filled with honey. We would find a banner hanging in front of the dwelling upon which was written in big letters "Herzlich Willkommen", a cordial welcome, a greeting which gave us just the right atmosphere as we took possession while mother began organizing the household. Mother's birthday happened in the summer, and these kind people always took great joy in helping us to decorate the cottage with ferns and flowers.

My sister Mathilde reminds me of something which perhaps affected her more closely, although it fascinated us as well. She made great friends with a daughter of our farmer landlords, a girl called Mirzl, whose hair was so gloriously red that if you saw her at a little distance you were conscious of a fiery glow rather than a human face. She was gay and charming and the friendship between her and Mathilde went so far that Mirzl always took Mathilde to church with her on Sunday mornings. It was highly important to the peasant girl that she should look what she thought thoroughly respectable on Sundays, and so she was always at great pains to hide her flaming red hair with a black head-scarf. Hairpins were apparently not enough to keep the scarf in place; and so Mirzl secured it firmly by sticking pins through the skin on her forehead, something that horrified Mathilde, who, like us, had not expected to meet an Indian fakir in the Salzkammergut.

Mirzl and her parents worked very hard during those summer months from sunrise to sunset—in the stables, in the fields, in the dairy making butter, looking after the bees, cutting firewood and carrying water.

The cottage water-supply charmed us. It came from a natural spring near by, the spring being protected by a delightful wooden casing designed and painted in the form of a doll's house. One lifted the roof to reach the water, which, while fresh, cool and sparkling, supported a little wild life in the way of a few black beetles or even a small snail or two, specimens of which we often carried home in the water-pails.

One summer we were given a baby lamb to look after. It had lost its mother at birth, a bereavement it suffered gladly in the joy of being with us. We put a little bell around its neck and it followed us everywhere, begging for titbits when it was not gambolling and playing in the full joy of living. We loved it so much that the thought of leaving it behind when autumn came was quite depressing. But as it turned out, autumn saw our endearing little woolly pet almost grown into a common sheep who rejoined the flock with as little regret as we felt in the parting.

We took great delight in helping the peasants in their farm work; but they never showed for a moment that we were in their way, allowing us to do odd jobs in the kindliest spirit.

Mother with the children always left Vienna in June, father following a month later and staying with us for a few weeks before going off with his brother or a friend on extensive sight-seeing tours, most often to Italy. His arrival was always the highlight of the summer holiday.

During the Aussee period we were still very young children, the eldest being eleven and the youngest only three; but hardly a day passed without father taking us out for walks in the forest. My mother's organizing genius was not apparent, but I think she had ruled that no child could join the expeditions with father until he was house-trained, or perhaps, one should say, forest-trained. Since it was felt that the presence of a governess or nursemaid on these delightful walks with father would add unwelcome constraint, the need for attention to this detail becomes obvious: my mother would never expect father to act as a nursemaid. As it happened, his expeditionary force could never boast more than five explorers of tender age.

Each outing was made an interesting adventure; but we all agreed that the most fascinating place was a clearing on the slopes of the Tressenstein, the steep, wooded hill at the foot of which our cottage stood. The clearing was called the Baerenmoos on one signpost and Beerenmoos on another, and thus it could have been translated on one signpost as the moor of the bears and on the other as the moor of berries, a lack of precision which aroused the indignation of my little brother Oliver, who had then only reached his second year at school. As we never met any bears but always found plenty of berries, Oliver should have been content with the berry version.

The Baerenmoos was perhaps only an ordinary kind of meadow somewhat isolated in a hilly forest; but, as an authority on psychology few would dare to question has confirmed, mine was a highly vivid imagination, and the clearing had for me an air of mystery and suspense, surrounded as it was by high fir-trees which shut out some light and occasionally left the area in semi-darkness. Mosses and ferns of many varieties flourished in abundance.

On the big leaves of some marshy plants we often saw salamanders of the most vivid black and yellow shades. They had an air of unreality. They could have been expensive advertisements, in their splendid shining colours, for a manufacturer of painted and lacquered goods. Father allowed it to be known that he thought they should be left in peace in their natural surroundings and not transferred to jam-jars, where he did not think they would be really happy.

To complete the mystery for me, the Baerenmoos had a forbidden corner, an upright chalk pinnacle rising a hundred feet from the dark-green forest and visible from a great distance, even from the balcony of our cottage. This chalk pinnacle had a name, the Daeumling, the little thumb.

Its structure was unstable, as chalk and rock always are, and it had, doubtless, been disintegrating for centuries. My sister, watching from a window of our cottage, once saw a large chunk of rock detach itself from the main structure and go thundering down the slopes of the Tressenstein. Around its base were lying odd bits of the Daeumling, some covered with moss and lichen, but still evidence of its slow disintegration, and its danger. Perhaps because father forbade us most strictly to go near the Daeumling, it exerted fascination.

That he was right was proved to me many years later when, ignoring his warning, I climbed the mysterious Daeumling with what might have been fatal results to a young woman relative and myself. I had become a grown-up young man staying with my Aunt Rosa, who had taken a charming Aussee cottage for the summer, my parents being somewhere else. Also staying with Aunt Rosa was my American cousin, Hella Bernays, who, having a Bernays for a father and a Freud for a mother, was really more a sister than a cousin to me. I was devoted to my Aunt Rosa, father's favourite sister, and Hella was a charming girl. The fact that my thoughtlessness might have brought tragedy into the happiest of atmospheres that summer has often made me shiver.

I decided to take Hella and Aunt Rosa's son, Hermann, to the top of the Daeumling. We reached the top in a few minutes, a great thrill for both because neither had ever attempted rock-climbing before; but during the descent a loop of the rope on which I had secured them caught just over my head on a pro-truding piece of rock, breaking off the rock, which came away and, after giving me a glancing blow with its sharp edges, thundered down, missing Hella by a few inches. Had that sharp piece of rock hit and cut the rope it is probable that Hella and I would have been killed or, at the least, very seriously hurt. As it was, she lost her foothold; but I was able to pull her back to safety. We lost no time in reaching the ground and, somewhat shaken, we withdrew to rest a safe distance from the Daeumling. My jacket and shirt were soaked with blood, but fresh blood-stains can be easily removed with cold water, and that evidence of the accident was hidden. The superficial cuts on my scalp offered more difficulty, but we found a surgeon who stitched them together, although he had to shave off the surrounding hair, which at that time was dark-brown and thick.

We decided to avoid all publicity so far as Aunt Rosa and her local contacts were concerned, and in this we were successful until, several days later, she asked why I, usually so polite, sat indoors with my hat on. I thereupon took off my hat and exposed the local damage. There was nothing in this story to amuse father, and I never told it to him.

I always feel, as I felt nearly sixty years ago, that our walks with father were much more exciting and entertaining than those enjoyed by other families. I was going to say that this was because they were so well organized; but the word will not do because it is a cold word; and our expeditions had the warmth of a delight-ful story which is well constructed and never lacking a good climax. The expeditions of young children led by our father, Sigmund Freud, always had a particular purpose: it might be searching for or collecting something, or it might be exploring some particular place. Often it would be the gathering of delicious wild berries of the woods; and since our holidays extended throughout the summer, we could cover the whole range of wild berries, beginning with wild strawberries and ending with the bilberries and blackberries of early autumn.

In late summer our subject was the collection of edible fungi; but we never discussed this with local people outside our circle. They would have thought the spending of many hours day after day gathering mushrooms a very dull business, something only poor old women did with big dilapidated baskets which they carried to the local market to earn a few kronen.

Every one could agree that fresh mushrooms made an excellent meal; but other fungi, very much like them, were poisonous and, it was true, few summers passed without visitors suffering from acute food-poisoning, occasionally fatal, after feasting on what they had picked as mushrooms. All of which seemed to them a good reason why wise people should leave mushrooms alone.

We had no fear. Father had taught us much about fungi, and I do not recall an occasion when we brought a poisonous species for him to inspect and pass as safe. There was nothing dull about these expeditions; on the contrary, we found them exciting and exhilarating, enjoying them not less than many enjoyed tennis, golf, shooting and other fashionable and expensive sports.

Our attack on the mushroom was never haphazard. Father would have done some scouting earlier to find a fruitful area; and I think one of the pointers he used was the presence of a gaily coloured toadstool, red with white dots, which always appeared with our favourite, the less easily seen *Steinpilz*, which my dictionary tells me is the yellow edible *boletus*. Once the area had been found, father was ready to lead his small band of troops, each young soldier taking up a position and beginning the skirmish at proper intervals, like a well-trained infantry platoon attacking through a forest. We played that we were chasing some flighty and elusive game; and there was always a competition to decide on the best hunter. Father always won.

Edible fungi vary a lot in size and even in shape, from the youngest which we called babies, small light-brown balls which hid themselves and were hard to detect, to the mature specimens which were flabby and often so large that a man's hat would not cover them. We called these *Alte Herren*, old gentlemen, and left them: their texture had lost firmness and there was no delicacy in their taste.

When I mentioned a man's hat, I had father's hat in mind, usually a grey-green velour hat with a wide dark-green silk ribbon. One sees these hats occasionally in England, where they are called Austrian hats. When father had spotted a really perfect fungi specimen, he would run to it and fling his hat over it before giving a shrill signal on the flat silver whistle he carried in his waistcoat pocket to summon his platoon. We would all rush towards the sound of the whistle, and only when the concentration was complete would father remove the hat and allow us to inspect and admire the spoils.

Mother's work began when we got home. Helped by her sister Minna, she would clean and skin the mushrooms before showing the cook precisely how they were to be cooked. In a good season we had mushrooms nearly every day; but we never tired of them.

These expeditions seldom, if ever, followed roads or pathways: they were made through wild forests and woods. We had to be dressed for these occasions, the boys always in boots and high thick stockings and leather shorts. When we got home the boys' stockings were thick with burs, and the skirts of the girls hardly less so. Since it was mother's job to get the stockings and skirts free of these, she occasionally complained, half-seriously, often wondering why we did not walk along decent pathways and expressing her belief that to follow us on our rambles one would need to have antlers, like a deer. This last remark invariably inspired arguments and disputes as we tried to explain to her that antlers would be a great nuisance, and not a help, to people slipping between trees and under low branches.

The question did not then arise; but when I look at old photographs of the ladies of my family I come to the conclusion that even with antlers to sweep aside obtruding branches, they would have had a hard job to follow us on our rambles in those woods and forests. With their long flowing skirts, their stiff collars gripping their necks and their laced stays forbidding all free movement, they could never have got over fallen trees; they could never had leapt across ditches, either wet or dry, and they would have been much too seriously encumbered to force their way through the bramble-infested dense undergrowth.

The ladies were not, however, conscious of the slightest disability, quietly enjoying their promenades on civilized pathways.

During those Aussee days, mother and her sister were really still quite young, in their early and middle thirties. Nowadays, women of their respectable middle class would think it quite normal to spend their summer holidays in an isolated cottage clad in slacks and pullovers with socks and sandals on their feet; and their hair might be cut short. I have insisted upon my vivid imagination as a boy, and even later in life; but my imagination could never stretch to the point of imagining my mother dressed in this way; and even if my imagination had broken away from wherever it sits in my head, its furthest flight could never take it high enough to picture Aunt Minna even on the warmest and sunniest days going about in shorts. Nothing could be more absurd, more utterly impossible, even approaching the sacrilegious. I knew Aunt Minna for the best part of my life, and I knew her very well; but I have never had any realization that she had legs.

There is another thing that has changed in holiday habits since my young days. Today, when people return from a holiday, they are always sunburnt; indeed that is the first thing one notices when they come back to the city, and it appears to be a good sign that they have enjoyed themselves. But in my young days when we lived in Vienna, when the line about mad dogs and Englishmen was still valid, people went for a holiday to escape the sun's heat in the towns. I cannot ever recall my parents or elders sunbathing.

However, when after three years at Aussee my parents decided on a change, it was not because of too much sunshine there: quite the reverse in fact; it was because of too much water, which in 1897 gave us an interesting if rather unpleasant experience when we saw a great flooding of the country.

It started, like the Biblical flood, with day after day of continuous rain, but not heavy enough to prevent our daily excursions; indeed, it was perfect weather for mushrooms although less pleasant to mother since we always returned water-logged and covered with mud. We wore *Lodencapes* over our ordinary clothes,

Martin Freud as a gunner in 1914 after gaining his first "Star" in the
Austrian Army

Sigmund Freud with his soldier sons, Martin and Ernst, 1916

Father, mother, Oliver's wife, and myself holding her little
daughter, Eva

squares of coarse woollen waterproof cloth with holes for our heads cut in their middles. The coarseness of this material made everything short of trees stick to it, so that we brought home half the forest—twigs, leaves, insects and even small snails, with all of which mother had to deal.

When eventually many paths and roads became flooded and each gentle stream became a raging torrent, our excursions had to be shortened. Bridge after bridge was washed away as the flood waters swept through the market town of Aussee and demolished a number of houses. At Obertressen, high above the valley and its river, we were comparatively safe, but a little lower down, houses had to be evacuated and the inhabitants with their cattle removed to safety.

Since most of our time was spent roaming with father in the forest, the music pavilion, in which a band usually played gay polkas and *Landlers*, had not interested us in the least; but when this pavilion, which stood on a hill, was used as a shelter for cattle refugees from the flooding—frightened beasts of all kinds, including cows, sheep, goats and even pigs all huddled together and protesting—we became more aware of the pavilion than we had ever been before. Even our Freudian lack of musical taste allowed us to know that the music of frightened beasts was less attractive than the gay polkas usually played in the pavilion.

Father always received a great amount of mail, even during his summer holidays with us; and he had made a special arrangement with the local postmaster that his letters should be delivered daily to our cottage, normally too far out of the way for the regular daily delivery. A small charge per letter was levied for this special duty, the postman keeping an account and being paid at regular intervals. One day when the flooding seemed at its worst, the postman said to father, "Herr Doctor, could we settle the account now: who knows whether or not we shall ever see each other alive again?" The postman was obviously a pessimist.

What clearly meant tragedy to the people of this area naturally awakened our sympathy, but without, in the case of us children, affecting our deep interest and the excitement we felt in watching the destructive power of water out of control. We were taken one day to a point of land from where, in perfect safety, we could watch the raging floods carrying all before them. We saw a solid-looking house at first dividing the rush of waters but gradually crumbling before their overwhelming power. When one corner of the ground floor had broken away, the shelves and counters of a general store were exposed. At that moment a powerfully built young man in leather shorts steered one of the flat-bottomed boats, common on the lake at Aussee, towards the stricken house; but when he was very near his objective he had had to drop his paddle for some reason or other, the result being that his boat was swung around by the current and he was carried away.

With many villages cut off through the collapsing of bridges, and some even flooded, particularly in the valley, the supply of food for our family soon became difficult, and my parents grew anxious as the larder became bare. The only safe exit from our cottage was a pathway leading over the hills and mountains, and this, in view of continuous rain, was exposed to landslides. To us Freud children the situation looked much blacker and more exciting than it probably was; but, undoubtedly, something had to be done if we were to be fed properly.

In these days, the most eminent citizens go shopping for groceries without gaining, or expecting, any sympathy; but when I was a boy, the very idea of a man in my father's position entering a shop to buy a pound or two of sugar would have been thought a highly undignified proceeding.

Thus it was that when father came down from his room one morning shouldering his biggest knapsack and dressed in the Norfolk jacket, knickerbockers, thick stockings and boots he used for forest expeditions, we were surprised: no plans had been made for a family expedition; but when we were told that he was about to begin a foraging expedition over the mountain road, in the hope of finding villages not affected by the flooding and with shops open, we decided that he was the most efficient, the wisest and most knowledgeable hero in the world. I recall to this day his expression of grim determination.

Father succeeded. He returned that evening with the great knapsack filled to bursting-point and obviously making a heavy burden. I cannot recall the contents but I do remember clearly that one important item was an enormous salami. I discussed this incident with my sister Mathilde the other day in London and she agrees about the big sausage. She cannot remember any other details: the salami evidently created a strong impression on us children.

We were, of course, eager to hear of father's adventures, because he had been away so long; but he, usually eager to entertain us, told us nothing: and this was clear evidence to us that he had had a pretty difficult time. Curiously enough, precisely the same conditions prevailed two years later at Berchtesgaden when a similar flooding cut us off from food supplies; and I have now got to admit, when I think of Berchtesgaden, that for the life of me I cannot be quite sure whether father's famous shopping expedition began from this latter place or from Aussee.

On one point I am perfectly sure: this is the only occasion I know of in Sigmund Freud's life when he went shopping for groceries.

It was in the summer of 1899 that we went to Berchtesgaden. It is, unfortunately, not necessary now to introduce the name of this lovely place to any one in the world. Forty years later, as all know, it became the centre of a reign of evil, and it must still remain for many a name of ill omen.

But be that as it may, Berchtesgaden is a place of unusual charm and long known in Germany as a mountain spa arranged suitably for the noble and very rich while still remaining attractive to the less noble and less rich. Tourists of all classes flocked in large numbers to Berchtesgaden from the German lowlands.

It was possible to rent cottages there, and father chose one on a hill away from the fashionable and crowded tourist quarters of the spa; indeed, its position was similar to that of the cottage at Aussee.

"The cottage is," father wrote to a friend, "a gem of cleanliness, loneliness and beautiful views; the women and children are happy in it, and look very well."

He wrote more particularly about his children from Berchtesgaden; and there is something touching when I look at our portraits: the children of forty years ago are, except for odd traits, so completely changed. "Little Anna", he wrote, "is positively beautified by naughtiness. The boys are already civilized members of society, able to appreciate things. Martin [myself] is a comical creature, sensitive and yet good natured in his personal relationships—completely wrapped up in a humorous world of fantasy of his own. When, one day, we passed a little cave in the rocks, he bent down and asked politely, 'Is Herr Dragon at home? No? Only Frau Dragon? Good morning, Frau Dragon! Has your husband flown to Munich? Tell him that I'll call again and bring him some sweets.' All this was occasioned by seeing the name Drachenloch [dragonhole] on a station between Salzburg and Berchtesgaden. Oli [my brother Oliver] makes plans of the mountains here just as he does with the underground lines and tramways in Vienna. They get on very well without any signs of jealousy."

In a letter written a few weeks later he said: "Conditions are ideal here, and I feel correspondingly well. I only go out mornings and evenings, and the rest of the time I sit over my work. On one side of the house it is always delightfully shady when the other is blazing hot. I can easily imagine what it is like in town.

"We find mushrooms daily. But on the next rainy day, I shall walk down to my beloved Salzburg; the last time I was there I picked up a few Egyptian things. These things cheer me and recall to my mind distant times and different countries."

Towards the end of August father wrote: "I have been here for four weeks now, and am regretting that this happy time is passing so quickly. In another four weeks my holiday will be over, and it is all too short. I have got on so well with my work here, in peace and with nothing to disturb me, and in almost complete health; and in between times I have gone for walks, and enjoyed the mountains and woods."

Mother was happy too. Although she had left Hamburg at the age of eight, she still spoke with a North German accent and born in her were the best Hamburg housewifely traditions which never permitted her to think very much of Austrian *Schlamperei*: a difficult word to translate, but I would say that it contains sloppiness and self-satisfied laziness.

Berchtesgaden is on the extreme southerly border of Bavaria where the people naturally hate and despise everything Prussian; but since the place had to cater for so many rich Prussians, what might be called a convenient Prussian spirit controlled the tradesmen and minor officials. Thus when a shoemaker promised to have children's shoes repaired at a certain time, the shoes were ready at the stroke of the hour. The same spirit controlled the butchers, the grocers and greengrocers. This met with mother's complete approval.

My mother had never lost her feelings of patriotic devotion to the Imperial German family, and it remains my impression, a memory not shared by my brother and sister who will not confirm it, that the hair style she selected for her own boys was strongly influenced by the one shown by the young princes. I remember the sons of Wilhelm II staying at Berchtesgaden while we were there and our meeting them on a promenade—a mother and her three sons: the Empress and three princes, and dressed very much as we were dressed, the Empress included, all chatting and talking together very much as we chatted and talked, as indeed the mothers and young sons of the not prominent people at Berchtesgaden behaved. Had we, I wondered, succeeded in imitating them; or were they imitating us?

Although my sister and brother will not confirm these slight contacts with the Kaiser's wife and sons, we all agree, as memory collectors, that we often bumped into a Wittelsbacher, a handsome and nice-mannered aristocrat, in the small swimming pool. I would not dare to say within hearing of my sister and my brother that this young man later became King of Bavaria; but I think that he did.

Like us, the aristocratic and rich wore traditional Bavarian costume, and many of the men would have looked very nice indeed if their legs had been less white and their knees less knobbly and slim. The general effect was a little ridiculous but not offensive.

However, Berchtesgaden was infested during its season with a much less attractive class of visitor, from the lower middle class of the German lowlands, Gevatter Schneider and Handschuhmacher, as Schiller called them in his drama, *Wallenstein*. These people behaved abominably enough to explain the unpopularity they won long before the world wars. They could never speak quietly, preferring to shout to each other at the top of their voices when they were not arrogantly quarrelling with the local people about fares, the cost of meals and even the price of local postcards. They appeared as ridiculous in the flesh as they appeared in caricature in the German comic periodical, *Simplicissimus.*

As fashion demanded, their women-folk wore long skirts: but to gain freer movement they wore girdles or belts round their waists from which dangled all the way around their bodies long straps, ending in clips which gripped the hem of the flowing skirts and drew them up to expose laced or buttoned walking boots reaching half-way up their calves, the boots armed with small loops at their backs designed to pull on the boots whose tops, now reaching coarse woollen stockings, mercifully ended the display.

We rented the house owned by a Bavarian and his mother, the latter a strong-minded, rather elderly woman who bossed her son about a good deal, so much indeed that it is more than likely she owned the property. She used to sit in a meadow in front of the cottage under an immense peasant umbrella capable of giving shade and keeping every drop of rain off her. She kept one eye on her cows and the other on her knitting: she was never idle.

The son was a *Herrgott-Schnitzer,* a wood-carver who specialized in carving the figure of Jesus on the Cross, a common art in Berchtesgaden, where it reached a high standard of perfection. During the summer season, he acted as guide; but this gave him little work because the only mountain tourists wanted to climb was the Watzman, to the top of which wound a serpentine pathway so well marked that a guide was unnecessary, even to people who do not really love mountains. The local guides were occasionally used as porters.

Mother once tried to use our landlord as a guide. Father with Uncle Alexander, the latter still a frequent visitor at our holiday resorts, had left early one morning on a walking and climbing expedition. When they had not returned at the time expected by mother, she became anxious. Having a general idea of the direction taken by father, she asked the guide to go and look for them and, she insisted, to go at once, since, she began to fear, they might be in danger.

But there is one thing you cannot do and that is to make a Bavarian hurry unless he feels like it, a fact never really accepted by mother, who should not have been surprised when our landlord dashed into his small cottage to wash his feet before he could go.

At the end of an hour he reappeared beautifully turned out in his professional outfit and ready to start.

However, at that moment we made out father and Uncle Alexander climbing up the hill to our cottage, and mother dismissed the guide.

We saw little of father during the summer holiday of 1899. He was absorbed in work which he could not neglect. This was his *Interpretation of Dreams*. It was unusual for him to discuss his work in the family circle; but this was something of an exception. We had all been told about it, and he even encouraged us to tell him of our dreams: something we did with enthusiasm. He even explained to us in simple language what could be understood of dreams, their origin and meaning. But I have promised not to write of my father's theories in this book, except when necessary; therefore, there will be no more about psychoanalysis and dreams. However, perhaps I might be permitted to say that he was disappointed when his book had a bad reception. The criticism was empty and the reviews inadequate. An ironic and malicious distortion of father's ideas threatened to kill the book.

I must add that this disappointment was never discussed and, in consequence, not felt at home. I learnt the facts years later, when I was quite grown up, when one edition followed the other and the work was recognized, and not only by his supporters, as opening up a new area in psychology.

## CHAPTER VI

W E spent the summer holidays of 1900 on the Bellevue; but I have already written of this. As late as the beginning of July 1901, nothing had been decided about our holiday.

Father wrote to his friend Dr Fliess: "I cannot say for certain yet where we are going. After all sorts of plans had miscarried, we hit on something unexpected, which will probably come off. I spent the two-day holiday at the end of June with Mama and Minna [Aunt Minna and her mother Emmeline] at Reichenhall and went on a carriage outing to the Thumsee, which is not far away, and lost my heart to the little place—with alpine roses coming right down to the roadway—a little green lake, magnificent woods all around, as well as strawberries, flowers and (we hope) mushrooms. I was so delighted with it that I asked whether or not there was any accommodation available at the only inn. I found that they were letting rooms there for the first time as the owner, a Bad Kirchberg doctor and property owner, who used to live there himself, had just died. So now negotiations are under way and will probably come off."

They did, in fact, come off; and we enjoyed a delightful summer with the little green lake, a most agreeable companion, of which I cannot give a better description than father gave in his letter. Reichenhall, the large and well-frequented spa near by with its salt-condensing plants, is recommended for diseases of the respiratory organs. Its reputation was international, but the great majority of its patrons were Hungarians.

The inn we occupied, more a café than an inn, was the goal of excursions made by the guests at the health resort who came for lunch or coffee, giving the place the status of an English tea-room, if less neat and tidy than the best English tea-rooms. This daily influx of visitors from Reichenhall did not greatly disturb our possession of the little green lake. They arrived; they drank their coffee or ate their luncheon; they bought picture postcards and wrote on them; they went to the shores of our little green lake and after throwing a few pebbles into its clear green waters and watching the fish for a few minutes, they often went off again, leaving us in sole possession of the small fleet of rowing-boats, in the handling of which we soon became expert. Our swimming improved very much too.

A high-road connecting Reichenhall with a less well-known part of the Bavarian Highlands ran along the side of the little oval-shaped lake opposite our lodging, and since the lake was only a few hundred yards wide, visitors approaching Thumsee from the high-road could be heard plainly if they shouted across to the café proprietor; and this they often did, bellowing their orders across the waters when just opposite the house, so that their meal might be ready for them when they had rounded the lake and arrived perhaps fifteen minutes later.

We did not think this showed very good manners; and it certainly disturbed the idyllic peace of Thumsee to hear shouts like "Paprika-goulash with dumplings for three, please!" being echoed and re-echoed from the surrounding hills.

We were a small family who loved tramping and exploring woods and forests; but the little green lake had no difficulty in seducing father and us from this delightful, if energetic, exercise. It was, as a matter of fact, a very hot summer; and so we spent most of our time boating, fishing and swimming. Father liked fishing and he enjoyed more success than his children. We used rods from the shore when we were not trawling from the small boats. Father was not fond of rowing, but he had plenty of eager oarsmen: one or two of us were always delighted to row while he trawled.

We made friends with a young American sportsman on holiday in the district, and a competition developed to see who could win the best sporting trophy in the way of fish and game. One day the young American returned in triumph from a hunting trip in the nearby mountains with a fat young roebuck in his rucksack. We were invited to admire this success which, we felt with a touch of jealousy, allowed the American to win the competition: something he felt quite sure of; but the next day, father caught a pike of unusually large size and the American was forced to admire the pike as we had admired his roebuck.

It was delightful, that summer at Thumsee; and it was largely delightful because we had father with us, a full member of our party, one who shared in our triumphs and disappointments, and I know that he was not playing a part, acting merely to please us. He was truly one of us, naturally and genuinely.

Unhappily, towards the end of our holiday there was an ugly and depressing incident which remains strongly marked in my memory. My brother Oliver and I were fishing one morning on the opposite side of the lake a few yards from the high-road which ran somewhat above the lake's level. A number of men had been watching us from the road, something which meant little to us, because fishermen are often watched by passers-by. We were shocked and considerably surprised when the men began abusing us, shouting that we were Israelites—which was true—that we were stealing fish—which was untrue—and being very offensive indeed.

We ignored them, refusing to reply; and we went on with our fishing. After a time, the men were met by other people with whom they marched off. Nevertheless, the joy in our fishing had gone and we returned home earlier than usual with less fish caught. We told father about it all, and he became very serious for a few moments, remarking that kind of thing could happen to us again, and that we should be prepared for it.

That same afternoon father had to go to Reichenhall and, as usual, Oliver and I rowed him across the lake to the highway to save him part of the walk. The men who had abused Oliver and me that morning were now reinforced by a number of other people, including women, and stood on the road near the primitive landing-place, apparently prepared to block the way to Reichenhall. As we moored the boat, they began shouting anti-Semitic abuse.

Father, without the slightest hesitation, jumped out of the boat and, keeping to the middle of the road, marched towards the hostile crowd. When he saw me following him, he commanded me in so angry a voice to stay where I was that I dared not disobey. My mild-mannered father had never spoken to me in anything but kindly tones. This display of anger, as I thought it, upset me more than all the abuse of the strangers. Nevertheless, I took an oar from the boat, swung it over my shoulder and stood by, ready to join any battle that might develop. It is unlikely that this armed reserve of one boy with an oar impressed the enemy very much. They numbered about ten men, and all were armed with sticks and umbrellas. The women remained in the background, but cheered on their men-folk with shouts and gestures.

In the meantime, father, swinging his stick, charged the hostile crowd, which gave way before him and promptly dispersed, allowing him a free passage. This was the last we saw of these unpleasant strangers. We never found out from where they came nor what their object had been in waylaying father.

This unpleasant incident made a deep impression on me; the impression was so deep that after more than fifty-five years I can still recall the faces of these crusaders in racial hatred. Time has, undoubtedly, distorted their outline but without blurring them; they remain fiendishly ugly. But there is no evidence that father was affected in the least. He never recalled the incident at home, and I am not aware that he ever mentioned it in any of his letters to our family or friends.

Towards the end of our holiday, father wrote to Dr Fliess: "I said I was also going to write to you about pleasant things. Thumsee really is a little paradise, particularly for the children, who are well fed here, fight each other and the visitors for the boats and then vanish on them from their parents' anxious eyes. Living among the fish has made me stupid, but in spite of that I have not yet got the carefree mind that I usually get on holiday, and I suspect that what is required is eight or twelve days in the land of wine and olive oil. Perhaps my brother will be my travelling companion."

This letter contradicts my memory of a superfluity of boats on the little green lake at Thumsee. Time has glorified and simplified those happy days of freedom, and I cannot recall, what is undoubtedly true, that visitors to the café did use boats and that occasionally there were not enough to go round amongst the lakefaring children.

Father duly left us at Thumsee and went with his brother to Rome, the fulfilment of a long and cherished wish and, as he wrote, a high spot in his life.

## CHAPTER VII

IN the spring of 1902, an event occurred in father's life which not only increased his earning capacity but also improved his social standing and that of his family. He was made a professor, a gesture long overdue since he had been *Privatdozent* since 1885. The term *Privatdozent* may not be familiar to some English readers. It is an honorary title given to the more promising young scientists and can be a step towards a professorship or other academic distinctions. The fact that father was a Jew was one reason for the delay; the other was that he was a pioneer in a new field of research looked upon by the leading men in psychiatry and psychology as fantastic, and even indecent. The title of professor now conferred on him did not, however, affect the attitude of the university's leading men: they continued to look down on the now middle-aged Jewish doctor and refused to take him seriously.

There can be no harm, perhaps, in repeating the often-told story of father's promotion. In 1897 he had been proposed as Professor Extraordinary to the University; but nothing had come of this. In 1900 a number of *Privatdozents*, until then overlooked for racial reasons, had been made professors and father left out again. He finally decided "to do something about it".

I might quote here from another letter to Dr Fliess, the last letter written to Dr Fliess before the end of a friendship of many years' standing; it refers to the professorship:

It was my own doing, in fact. When I got back from Rome, my zest for life and work had somewhat grown and my zest for martyrdom had somewhat diminished. I found that my practice had melted away, and I withdrew my last work from publication because, in losing you, I had lost my only remaining audience. I reflected that waiting for recognition might take up a good portion of the remainder of my life, and that in the meantime, none of my fellow-men were likely to trouble about me. And I wanted to see Rome again and to look after my patients and to keep my children happy. And so I made up my mind to break with my strict scruples and to take appropriate steps, as others do, after all. One must look somewhere for one's salvation, and the salvation I chose was the title of professor.

The first attempts to gain a professorship failed. Here again I quote from the same letter:

Then another force came into play. One of my patients heard about the matter and went into action on her own. She did not rest until she had made the Minister's acquaintance at a party; she made herself agreeable to him and secured a promise through a mutual woman friend that he would give a professorship to the doctor who had cured her. But being sufficiently well informed that a first promise from him meant nothing at all, she approached him personally, and I believe that if a certain Boecklin had been in her possession instead of in that of her aunt, I should have been appointed three months earlier. As it is, His Excellency will have to satisfy himself with a modern picture for the gallery which he intends to open, naturally not for himself. Anyway, in the end, the Minister most graciously announced to my patient while he was having dinner at her house that the appointment had gone to the Emperor for signature, and that she would be the first to hear when the matter was completed.

Finally father wrote:

I have obviously become reputable again, and my shyest admirers now greet me from a distance in the street.
I myself would gladly exchange five congratulations for one good case coming for extensive treatment. I have learnt that the old world is governed by authority just as the new is governed by the dollar. I have made my first bow to authority, and am entitled to hope to reap my reward. If the effect in a wider circle is as great as in the immediate one, I may well hope so.
In the whole affair there is one person with very long ears, and that is myself. If I had taken these few steps three years ago, I should have been appointed three years earlier, and should have spared myself much. . . .

This is an old story of an amiable intrigue of which, naturally enough, a boy of twelve could know nothing; but I knew my father well enough to be certain that had he known of his grateful patient's plans beforehand, what he called "a compulsion to

honesty which was so detrimental to my interests" would have
urged him to protest and to call a halt to the negotiations. In
fact the negotiations were more gracious than even the slightest
bit sinister, and father could accept the *fait accompli* with com-
posure and only the lightest of conscience-pricking. In any case,
that was the way things were arranged in Austria of that day.
The bribe, a painting by Boecklin, considered one of the master-
pieces of the century, was not given to the Minister. It was taken
from comparative obscurity in a private collection and placed in
a public gallery to be opened by the Minister, where it could be
admired by the art-loving Viennese.

And the briber, Baroness Marie Ferstel, whose name is already
exposed in my father's biography, thus permitting me to mention
—what I would not otherwise mention—the briber, had no selfish
motives. Her motives were those of gratitude and friendship. She
was, incidentally, the wife of the architect who had designed the
Votivkirche.

But we children knew nothing about this background to my
father's appointment as a professor, a background so well justified
by events and somewhat pathetic in retrospect: because why
should even amiable intriguing have been necessary? All we
knew was that a warm friendship existed between my parents and
the Ferstels, something in which we shared: because the families
exchanged visits and we were often invited to a Christmas party
at the home of the Baroness where a great Christmas-tree with
precious presents spread below it gave an atmosphere of luxury
and wealth to which we were not accustomed. We knew that
these people moved in a higher class of society than ours, but we
were too young, or too unsophisticated, to be the slightest bit
impressed by that. I, being highly impressionable, immediately
fell in love with the eldest daughter; she was my own age, with
wavy black hair.

Upon one occasion, the Baroness took the two eldest of us to
the Burgtheatre, one of the two Viennese theatres supported by
the Emperor, to see a performance of Schiller's *William Tell*. We
sat in great comfort and luxury in the baronial box. At the end
of the performance my sister, doubtless, thanked our hostess
correctly for an enjoyable time. I, according to my sister—I have
no recollection of the incident myself—was so carried away by

the beauty of the drama and the kindness that had inspired the Baroness to invite us, that I leapt into her arms and kissed her fervently. My sister does not remember the effect on the Baroness; but from what I remember of the latter, I think she understood perfectly how I felt.

One memorable day the Ferstels came to dinner with our parents and this was one of the occasions when we had chicken, which my mother never served except when we had guests, because of my father's dislike of it. I sat very near the Baron at the long table beautifully laid by my mother, finding myself fascinated by his long, beautifully manicured, aristocratic hands which, I felt, were not really useful members when I saw him offered chicken by the servant. Instead of taking a succulent piece of the breast from the variety of portions on the plate, the beautiful hands took up a piece which seemed only skin and bone. I was eager to advise him on a much better choice, but being hushed into silence by a frown from my mother, I had to content myself with waiting until the guests had gone to get an explanation of this extraordinary conduct.

My mother said that the Baron had not been stupid. He had been polite and showed good manners: a well brought-up guest, she explained, always helped himself as modestly as possible, leaving the better portions for those who came after him.

I understood and admired without ever being tempted to live up to so aristocratic a rule.

## CHAPTER VIII

T HE year was now 1902, and father was in his middle forties. But although his face showed signs of strain through over-work and deep mental concentration, his body remained astonishingly young, strong and agile; he still moved with the speed and lightness of youth.

I was entering the uneasy and awkward stage of adolescence. I no longer fancied myself as a poet quite so much although, only a few years earlier, I had signed my letters "Dichter M. F."— Poet Martin Freud. Incidentally, the misfortune suffered by bio-graphers of my father when correspondence ceased between him and his former great friend, Fliess, has one facet which, at this stage of my life, interests me. These letters contained much valu-able information about Freudian theories as they developed. They also contained carefully, and pridefully, transcribed copies of the poems written by his eldest son, by me, Martin Freud. I have re-read this verse in the original letters. Only a few appeared in *The Origin of Psychoanalysis*. Of course it is true that few authors reread their work without at least some pain, or embarrassment, and it is natural enough for me to have found nothing either remarkable or original in my poetic efforts, even if I could recall the exaltation I enjoyed in their glowing birth. Regarding them calmly and critically now, I reach the safe conclusion, not denied by the tactful silence of others, that really to appreciate my verse it is not enough to be its author: one must be the poet's father. That, of course, tends to limit a poet's audience.

We were now a professor's family, commanding more respect from landlords and traders than we had enjoyed before father's promotion.

Our parents had found us a comfortable house this summer on a hill only ten minutes' walk from the shores of the famous Koenigsee, near Berchtesgaden. We occupied this during the three following summers. It was a square, solid, whitewashed building called Villa Sonnenfels, and it was owned by a baker, who still occupied for his trade one side of the ground floor, the baker's

Father with his daughter, Anna

Myself back in uniform in 1934 as a Lieutenant in the
Austrian Artillery

Martin Freud as a private in the Pioneer Corps, 1941

Sigmund Freud with two young chows

shop in fact, behind which was the actual bakery. Since no part of the place was out of bounds to us children, we soon became friendly with the baker and learnt many of the secrets of bread-making, indeed everything except the mixing of the yeast and the preparing of the dough, which began late at night when we were all sound asleep. The baker had a steady and prosperous trade, and my memories of those three summers are pleasantly associated with the ringing of a little bell attached to his door which announced to the bakery that a customer had arrived in the shop. The customers were largely barefooted children under school age who had come from the village of Koenigsee, carrying in their small dirty hands crumpled slips of paper with a shopping order.

Koenigsee had everything to make a summer holiday pleasant for both parents and children, and we thoroughly enjoyed the three years we spent there. There were long walks through beautiful pine forests with berries and mushrooms. We could reach entrancing mountain scenery by taking short walks and climbs from the villa: there was easy access to the region of Alpenrosen and, for the first time in our lives, we could find edelweiss on the steep and rocky slopes of the mountain dominating the scene, the Brett, the board, so called from its shape. Then there was the lake, only a few minutes' walk downhill on a foot and cycling pathway, with swimming, fishing and boating.

The Koenigsee is famous for the grandeur of its setting in superbly lovely mountain scenery; it is surrounded almost everywhere by high mountains whose sides drop sharply to its waters. The only flat shore within anything like convenient distance of our villa was at its northern end where its waters prepare to form a lively quick-flowing river leading to the valley of Berchtesgaden. It was to this small beach that the pathway from our villa led.

The small area of flat land was naturally valuable here, being fully taken up by hotels, jetties, boat-houses and pavilions where postcards and souvenirs were sold. From this beach a pathway led around a sharp corner of the lake to a point from where a fine view could be gained.

During the summers we were there, only a few bathing-huts remained at this end of the lake, near the boat-houses which, in turn, were close to the lake's flood-gates. They were not often used then, and I noticed when I visited this spot some years later that they had been taken away. They stood on piles in the water a yard or two from the shore, to which they were connected by a narrow board bridge. They differed from the bathing-huts which, I understood, were common on British beaches at that time. They were designed to permit modest ladies to enter the water in complete privacy. These Bavarian bathing-huts had a platform along one side upon which people could stand to undress and to hang their clothes on the pegs which were furnished. The other side of the hut was a trough with, at the lake end, a round opening like the porthole on a ship. Through this the water of the lake flowed, the porthole being only half submerged to permit a certain degree of lighting in the otherwise dark hut. The water in the trough was usually not more than three feet deep, enough to permit the ladies to paddle discreetly and even to wash, since soap was permitted.

These portholes supplied an exit from the imprisonment of the restricted wooden huts more suitable for seals, or even for half-grown boys who could dive a bit, than for adult persons of both sexes, particularly if they enjoyed the average Bavarian proportions of chest and belly. The huts were supposed to give full privacy, and the use of bathing-costumes was not prescribed. They were not worn. The authorities did not think the portholes affected privacy.

Father never dreamt of using these old-fashioned huts, and the only member of the family ever to use one was Mathilde, who apparently enjoyed a splash on very warm days. I know that most females avoided the huts because little fish used to swim merrily over the floor boards of the troughs, alarming the ladies as mice do on land.

Since what was to be called "mixed bathing" was still beyond the horizon of that period, it would not have been considered proper for me to bathe with my sister even from the open beach; and so I found a friend, a young Bavarian of my own age, whose family had a villa in the neighbourhood. We argued and quarrelled a good deal but remained good friends.

There was a small island, towards the middle of the lake, off the point of mountainous land where the lake turned, and from where its glorious panorama of beauty could be enjoyed. This island was called Cristliger, in honour of a Roman Catholic saint,

St John Nepomuk. The statue of the saint rose up from the dense vegetation which crowded the small islet. Since landing on it was strictly forbidden to everybody, it naturally exerted great fascination for my friend and me. The distance not being great, and both of us being strong swimmers, we often tried to swim it. But no matter how low we kept in the water, no matter how carefully and without splashing we swam, we never succeeded in getting far without being seen by the elderly, but falcon-eyed, master and owner of the Koenigsee boats. Much as he was preoccupied with people hiring boats and getting started—always a rather unruly scene—he never failed to hurl at us strong shouts which sent us back to the shore. We never reached the small island, but like true explorers, we never abandoned hope of getting there one day.

We were both of an age when curiosity about the facts of life, with some emphasis on the female form, then so heavily disguised and even distorted by the prevailing fashions, allowed us to wonder out loud to each other just what was hidden by all these frills and furbelows. My friend had, of course, seen the many statues of stately nude ladies in bronze, marble, masonry or stucco, many bearing aloft candelabra, which adorned his home city of Munich. Vienna, being similarly decorated, placed our discussions on a level. I recall summing up my attitude by saying, "No real lady would appear in public like that," adding that I thought the display of sculpture in both cities nothing but a swindle.

Our discussions were, of course, inconclusive and, in consequence, our curiosity remained. An opportunity to satisfy it came one day, and we seized upon it.

Two tall, red-headed Bavarian *Dirndls* (young girls) had occupied the bathing-hut next to ours, and when we heard sounds which suggested they were preparing for a dip, we decided to dive through our porthole, to swim out a little way and then to return, taking a quick peep through the porthole of theirs. We had not, however, reckoned with the beach-master's excellent knowledge of morbid adolescent curiosity. He saw what we were up to at once, ordering us back quite rudely and threatening to tell our parents. The threat seriously alarmed my companion,who knew how heavily he might be punished; he panicked and raced back through the water to our hut without a single glance. I was less frightened and, while ostensibly obeying the beach-master, I took a quick glance through the porthole and rejoined my nervous friend.

The girls were standing on the platform quite unclothed, but the picture they offered was not fascinating to my eyes. They were long, thin, white and angular, even bony, I thought, with no suggestion of seductive curves. Today I might think their heads of glorious red hair enchanting; but then this glory had no effect on me. I said to my friend, "I saw them: it's all a swindle. Girls with their clothes off are just like boys with their clothes off. It's nothing but a swindle," I repeated. Incidentally, we never bothered to decide who wanted to swindle us.

The beach-master's threat had not alarmed me in any way. I think my father would have laughed had he been told. I remember, however, that before this quite shocking incident there had been a discussion in the family about cattle when it became clear to father that none of his children knew the difference between a bullock and a bull. "You must be told these things," father had exclaimed; but, like the majority of fathers, he had done nothing whatever about it. If the beach-master had reported our escapade, he might have been forced to explain.

Bathing and swimming played really only a minor part in the programme of our entertainment; the Koenigsee waters were very cold and only attractive on hot days. But we enjoyed much fishing of what might be called a primitive kind because little money was spent on our fishing gear. With sometimes four or five in a boat, conventional rods with reels and so on would have been impracticable: we would have got in each other's way. As it happened, hazel rods we ourselves cut, with enough line attached and baited with worms sufficed for the children, even if father, and sometimes uncle, had something more professional. Our luck varied; I thought the curious attitude of mothers was illustrated one day when, having been accompanied by father and uncle, we caught a big load of perch. Father and uncle were highly excited when we reached home; but mother became very cross, complaining that there were not enough frying-pans to deal with the fish nor enough mouths to eat such a haul.

On most days, the Koenigsee was perfectly safe for bathing; but on rare occasions fierce squalls could develop, and if these blew along the length of the narrow lake, unruly waves would rise which could play havoc with the punt-like boats with their very low freeboard. I might mention here that at this time the lake and the surrounding land belonged to the Wittelbachers, the royal family of Bavaria, and they had had the aesthetic sense to forbid any traffic on the lake driven by steam, oil or electricity.

The boats used by tourists were propelled by the manly and womanly *élite* of the neighbouring village, a man standing at the stern to steer rather like a gondolier while one or two women sat like galley slaves propelling the boat with oars. The passengers sat on seats facing each other. In addition there were conventional rowing-boats on the lake.

Since for long distances the land met the water in steep walls of rock, a boat caught in a fierce mountain squall was in great danger since it was literally impossible to land. I was told of one of these boats manned, or womanned, by women only, that was caught in a storm. Soon it was driven helplessly against a rocky wall which, fortunately, offered a few sparse and scraggly trees and other vegetation sprouting through narrow cracks in the rocky wall. The boatwomen clung desperately to branches and bushes, trying to prevent their boat from being smashed against the rocks as it began filling rapidly. Since none of them could swim, they began shrieking for help. Their cries were heard and soon a boat, driven by four members of the most powerful rowing team in the district, set out boldly to their aid. The rescue boat reached the women's water-logged vessel in the nick of time; indeed it sank to the bottom of the lake a few seconds after the last female was dragged to safety. I swallowed this story (told to me by a local man) hook, line and sinker without thinking to ask how a wooden punt could sink to the bottom of even the Koenigsee, but this detail is unimportant because I knew that undoubtedly there had been tragedies during these storms.

At one part of the lake the particularly steep rocky wall was thickly adorned with *Marterls*, sinister and beautiful to my easily impressed mind. Because some people may not know what a *Marterl* is, I had better explain that in this part of Bavaria it was, and probably still is, the custom to mark the scene of a fatal accident by something resembling a small shrine, a square foot of board upon which a touching picture is painted illustrating the accident and topped by a saint enthroned in clouds. Usually a little verse or two is added and a request to passers-by to pray for the soul of the victim who had died without the consolation of religion.

We Freud children were always deeply interested in *Marterls*, never failing to pause near any we met, sadly to study the picture and to read the poetry which I, being a poet myself, always thought excellent, even as good as some of my own. Secretly I hoped that one day I might be called upon to devise a verse of this kind: not that I could contemplate any tragedy without the deepest melancholy; it was merely that if, unhappily, anything very dreadful came along, I was there with my poet's soul to meet it beautifully.

Actually, however, I was greatly relieved to escape this melancholy duty when Uncle Alexander, having ventured out alone on the Koenigsee in a rowing-boat, was caught in a storm and might easily have been drowned. Incidentally, the distinct differences in personality between father and my uncle were never shown more clearly than when they talked of any adventures they endured or enjoyed. Father was *wortkarg*, laconic (a near enough translation if not a perfect one), and he seldom told of his adventures even when he had suffered hardship and had overcome serious danger, although he might write of such to an intimate friend. On the other hand, all incidents were grist to Uncle Alexander's mill, and a story of the Emperor's reception of a prime minister reporting a critical situation, and perhaps what he thought about a performance of *Cavalleria Rusticana* by a third-rate company in a small provincial town would each receive the same glowing and elastic treatment. All uncle's tales were vivid; all the people in them came alive, and we children always listened enthralled.

Punctuality for meals was an iron rule in the *ménage* controlled by my mother. Thus, when Uncle Alexander was several hours late for one, we feared the worst, not being entirely surprised when he eventually returned worn out and exhausted. It was clear that he would have a wonderful story to tell and everybody gathered round him.

The story of his struggle in the rowing-boat as he fought the unruly waves was of his best. He personified the waves until I, the most impressionable of his audience, saw them and heard them developing their conspiracy to drown him.

"Now watch me," said one haughty wave to her sisters; "I am going to smash this flimsy boat against the rocks." "You leave it to me," said another; "I saw it first." "But let's look at the man in the boat," suggested another, as she splashed a few buckets full of Koenigsee water over uncle's knees; "believe me or not," she cried after a short glance, "he hasn't even taken off his shoes. This is a provocation; does he think we won't be able to capsize his boat?" "Let him keep his shoes on," said another wave dashing up at speed; "what difference will that make? He is probably a poor swimmer who will drown as comfortably in his shoes as he would with them off."

As uncle told his story, I could not only hear the waves chattering fiercely, but I could also see him, a short stocky figure, now fighting for his life, as he, a poor student, had fought life and won influence and wealth. Our teeth chattered as we saw uncle fighting his way past the most dangerous points in his adventure, past the sombre wall so densely decorated with *Marterls*, each one telling of a lost fight.

Indeed, as in imagination I saw the *Marterls* above the unruly waves threatening to drown poor Uncle Alexander, I also saw myself being commissioned to paint and compose his *Marterl*, when the name Alexander Freud would offer a contrast to all the Sepp Obereggers, Modereggers and Angerers of the *Marterls* already in residence on that rock wall above the generally quiet waters of the Koenigsee. Perhaps, I felt, I would have to offer my services as not only a near relative of the victim, but also as the celebrated youthful poet and painter whose reputation had been built up by Professor Sigmund Freud. And then came a depressing thought: perhaps authority might sponsor local talent.

Even while a dream-drowned Uncle Alexander, in fact as large as life and with, to us children, five times the charm of all the lives in the world, even while he went on telling his story, I saw objections to an Alexander Freud *Marterl* on that rocky wall. It is, apparently, *de rigeur* to have a saint enthroned amidst clouds painted on the *Marterl* and, in addition, it is equally important to ask those who pass to say prayers for the repose of the victim's soul. In consequence, *Marterls* might be reserved only for Christian victims.

Of course, the chief objection to my being commissioned was

the undoubted fact that Uncle Alexander had, happily even to the mind of morbid adolescence, escaped safely and was sitting next to me tucking into a belated and copious meal, undoubtedly replacing all the weight he may have lost in his fight against the elements.

We became well-known in the small village of Koenigsee and made many friends. Always when we walked together down the footpath leading to the lake, the children ran to their gates to greet us by name: "Mathilde, Martin, Oliver——" They remembered them from one summer to the other. The older people enjoyed telling us stories, a favourite being the rescue of the Amazons I mentioned earlier; but most of the stories were of startling incidents between poachers and gamekeepers, the poacher invariably being the hero and the gamekeeper the villain of these epics.

The baker's son, of about our own age, was our very best friend. Our parents, who approved of this friendship, often took him with us on excursions. He wore the same kind of local dress Oliver, Ernst and I wore: leather shorts and broad green braces, except that his braces were nicely embroidered with edelweiss and the slogan "Gott Schuetze Bayern"—God Save Bavaria. One afternoon when he was with us, we had refreshments at a fashionable café at the Salzberg (where Hitler lived later). As a very special treat at this time, mother ordered ice-creams for all of us; and when we asked Toni (for that was the boy's name), who had never tasted ice-cream before, how he liked his he replied, much to father's amusement, "A good food, but a painful one."

My sisters were more selective in their friendships. Once when they were asked why they did not play with the daughter of a ranger who lived near by, a sweet and pretty little girl, they replied demurely that they had made the shocking discovery when playing with her on the swings that she did not wear drawers.

# CHAPTER IX

DURING the Koenigsee period, when father was still under fifty and, with the exception of Anna, all the children in their teens, we were able to form a quick-moving team of eager mountaineers.

I have mentioned earlier that Sigmund Freud was extremely fond of alpine flowers, but I do not think I have given pride of place in his heart to the *Kohlroeserl* (*Nigritella nigra*), a small dark-purple flower, almost black, with a peculiarly strong and sweet perfume. Although I recall finding a meadow at a high altitude in the Engadine alive with these flowers, they are rare in the Austrian and Bavarian mountains. Father never explained his preference for *Nigritella nigra*, but we all knew why he liked them; indeed it would have been extremely difficult in our family not to know because every time we brought these flowers home mother told a story, not a dramatic story, perhaps not even an important one to any one but herself: it was simply that when she was still a bride she had been on the Schneeberg with her young and handsome husband and they had spotted a clump of these flowers. He had climbed a steep, grassy slope to gather some for her. Throughout her life, until she was driven from Austria, the sight and the scent of the *Kohlroeserl* brought back this happy period in her life.

Although father loved climbing and had a flair for it, it would not be true to say that he was a good mountaineer: he started too late in life, too late to appreciate what might be called the rigour of the game; and he showed the faults of all eager beginners, notably that optimistic attitude of mind towards snow-bridges, towards hidden crevasses in glaciers, to exposed ravines upon which rocks can crash and towards shrubs growing out from steep rock faces. I think it is true to say that a good mountaineer will never take a chance if a chance can be avoided. I began climbing at the age of eight and I have learnt that all mountains of interest to climbers are worthy of deep respect and not a little suspicion. Quite a number of my friends, all optimists in this respect, have lost their lives, and, I think, sometimes needlessly.

I would not have dared to express these thoughts to father during our glorious Koenigsee days even if I had been old enough to think them, even when he gave a display of optimism in climbing from which he escaped very neatly, although, I now know, he could easily have broken his neck.

Father was leading a small expedition consisting of four of us, including Sophie, the youngest of the party. All was going well when someone thought he detected *Kohlroeserl* growing somewhat high above us on a steeply graded mountain meadow beyond a high barrier of rock rising to about thirty feet. Father at once took off his rucksack and began climbing, all of us watching with due admiration, although, it must be admitted, little Sophie seemed far from happy.

Father was doing very well. Indeed, his hands had reached to within a few feet of the almost perpendicular rock face when he made a false move. A bush of *Alpenrosen*, apparently quite strong, seemed capable of taking much of his weight and thus to allow a final pull which would take him to the top. Father was disagreeably deceived. The roots of the *Alpenrosen* were not strong. Little Sophie shrieked in horror and anxiety as father began falling backwards followed by the *Alpenrosen* and a shower of earth and small stones. Much to our admiration, father achieved a beautifully co-ordinated movement of his body which produced a back somersault, like a diver leaving a springboard, and Sophie's concern, which he felt, or may have noticed, allowed him to burst into a hearty guffaw of laughter, even before he came out of the somersault, and to continue laughing when he landed safely on his feet with no more harm than a triangular rent in his knickerbockers. Sophie, like most children, was hard to deceive but, again like most children behaving nicely when out with father, she was willing to be deceived on behalf of tact; and she joined in our merriment with only slight reserve. However, for the rest of that day she clung tightly to father's hand.

There is a proverb in the Alps: *"Auf der Alm da gibts ka Suend"*—there is no sin on an *Alm*. An *Alm* is an area of pastureland fairly high up on a mountain-side where cattle are taken to graze during the summer months, where the cowherds live in small log cabins, making butter and cheese, following the same methods of production that might have been followed a thousand years ago. They work very hard, but they have also time to play hard, enjoying a merry life remote from authority, in full appreciation, it is said, of their proverb.

During many years of mountaineering, I have paused at *Alms* in Austria, Bavaria, Switzerland and Italy, the last-named, incidentally, making an unpleasant contrast so far as cleanliness is concerned with the Austrian and Bavarian.

One day during a holiday at Koenigsee, it was arranged that the three boys in the family should ascend to an *Alm* above the Koenigsee. To reach this *Alm* it was necessary to take a boat about half-way along the lake to a landing-place from where climbed a bridlepath leading to the *Alm* about twelve miles distant. This water journey, entirely necessary since there was no other access to the *Alm*, gave the excursion added romance. Father did not go with us: he had got beyond the age when one can enjoy sleeping in hay-lofts and similar adventures. Our landlord, the baker, had volunteered to chaperone us and he took along with him his first journeyman, a nice young fellow and always a good friend to us boys.

We found a woman was in charge of this *Alm*, which is usual in Bavaria; in Switzerland, a man most often is the leader. The woman of the Koenigsee *Alm* was of immense proportions, still fairly young and nice-looking in her way. She was to my young eyes a perfect Teutonic Valkyrie, a battle-maiden of Odin whose job in Teutonic mythology was to conduct warriors slain in battle to Valhalla. My impression was that if this woman had been called upon to pick up three or four slain warriors *en route* for Valhalla, she could have carried them there without the slightest difficulty. I watched with awe this *Sennerin*, the official name for her rank and occupation, carry without effort an enormous blackened copper kettle to the open fireplace.

No other heroic duties were expected of the *Sennerin*, however; indeed, she concentrated her attention on my small brother Oliver with so much tenderness and care that Oliver became embarrassed and far from co-operative. Oliver had by now lost that prettiness which had won the hearts of all in former years, but he was still quite attractive. In her broad Bavarian accent, she offered him local food—milk, *Sterz* (local porridge) and *Speck* (smoked bacon); but he refused everything with so much determination and so clear an air of hurt pride since, he felt, this great big woman was treating him as a baby, that we all, including the baker and his boy, laughed. The *Sennerin*, on the other hand, found these refusals depressing and she looked quite sad, so sad, indeed, that there was some danger of her flinging her mighty arms around Oliver and smothering him in a warm, if unthinking, hug.

My impression is that little Oliver was less frightened of the unusual food the *Sennerin* offered than of her trousers. None of us had ever before seen a woman in trousers, but while this fascinated me, it shocked Oliver. I studied the trousers closely, which was easy, because they were so big. They were of blue denim and fitted tightly, held in position by buttons on each side of the waist, and they reached to about half-way down the *Sennerin*'s legs. Indeed, looking back on them over the years, I would say that they followed almost precisely the cut of jeans, apparently beloved by modern teenage members of the fair sex. There was one difference: the *Sennerin* did not depend on the buttons to keep her trousers in place: on behalf of safety-first, she wore strong braces. I might remark that while alpine jeans were accepted on the *Alm*, they would not be tolerated in the valley; and without doubt our big girl would have to hide her monumental calves under the chaste folds of a dirndl when she returned to her home village.

Our little party, the baker, his assistant and us three boys, were alone with the *Sennerin* at first, but as the day's work ended, visitors began arriving. Life on the *Alms* is highly social and soon we had dairy-maids, farm servants from other log cabins in the vicinity and rangers from the forest to join us. They all wore the picturesque alpine costume, quite naturally of course, for the simple reason that they did not own any other kind of clothing any more than had their ancestors for countless generations.

Finally, with the arrival of the last caller, a jolly and handsome ranger who was obviously a local favourite, the already homely and friendly atmosphere of the hut changed to noisy gaiety. One visitor had a zither and the baker's boy had brought a guitar on his back; and so with music and song the party developed to the delight of all concerned except, eventually, of the three small boys whose curiosity in the gay behaviour of these grown-ups was soon satisfied as they began to feel somewhat sleepy. The *Sennerin*, on the other hand, showed no signs of weariness. She was transformed as the company of handsome men around her fire increased to the size of a platoon. She became lively as her eyes sparkled and her face flushed: she had assumed the position of a beauty queen, forgetting all about little Oliver who had been so unresponsive to her charms.

There was no chimney in the hut, and since the smoke had to get out somehow, it began settling in our unaccustomed eyes, enough to make us want to get out into the fresh air, although, to tell the truth, we felt that three small boys were really *de trop* in this gay company of grown-ups. The kind baker, sensing our discomfort, led us to a hay-loft and gave each of us a coarse blanket.

The hay was not sweet and fresh; indeed it was dry and some-what dusty perhaps because of the good warm weather they had been enjoying on the *Alm*; but the night was mild and streams of lovely fresh air blew through the loft, a blessing after the hot smoky atmosphere of the hut. We took off our boots but kept our clothes on, regretting that our leather shorts left our bare knees to be tickled and slightly pricked by the hay. However, we rolled ourselves in our blankets and settled down to sleep. My impression was that my blanket had recently belonged to a hard-working horse or mule, I could not guess which, because I presume their respective sweats smell very much the same. I blamed my un-usually keen sense of smell, not shared by my brothers, and so decided not to upset them by discussing the subject.

I do not know what my brothers thought about this night in the hay-loft, but my own feelings were that while it was interest-ing and romantic, it was also rather uncomfortable. And while I would not have missed the adventure for the world, I decided that perhaps it was a very good thing that the experience was unique and not likely to be repeated.

How wrong I was! When the First World War came, sleeping on hay, on straw, on hard boards and even on the bare earth became an everyday experience for all of us.

Throughout that night we could hear the cattle below us getting along in their limited surroundings, chewing, snorting and staggering about, but we heard no cow-bells and we wondered why. Since to us in a vague way a cow-bell was as much a part of a beast as its horns or tail, the question became of great importance as we asked ourselves why the bells were not ringing. One brother suggested that perhaps the cattle did not wear bells in their bedroom. The question became so urgent that eventually we felt bound to ask the baker, also curled up in the hay; but when I crept up to him I found he was snoring and I did not dare to awaken him to ask, "Do cows sleep with their bells on?" We decided to let the question sleep with us, and to awaken it with ourselves in the morning. As it happened, the question remained asleep, because we forgot all about it; and it is still asleep after fifty years. Since I now live in a country where, so far as I know, cows never wear bells, I have no means of finding out and so the question, "Do cows sleep with their bells on?" remains open so far as I am concerned.

Father spent much time writing during our holidays at Koenigsee, remaining indoors in the Villa Sonnenfels instead of following his usual practice of spending most of his time with us children. However, we were growing old enough to amuse ourselves. I recall one incident which I might label "The Rock of Disappointment" with perhaps wry amusement, something I did not feel at the time.

A few minutes' walk from the villa a high isolated rock stood in a grove, probably a relic of a great landslide of prehistoric times. It was roughly square with a flat top and it stood about twenty-five feet high. The walls were fairly steep, steep enough to forbid casual climbing; and thus the flat top, towards which we often saw squirrels running, assumed to us the mystery of the unknown and unexplored. There were no signs to show that any human being had ever attempted to climb that rock to sit in the shade of the few meagre kinds of tree that adorned the summit. We Freud children often played in this grove around the rock, picking bilberries in the late summer and often marching around the mysterious pinnacle, gazing at its top with great curiosity.

One day I decided to climb this rock. There were enough crevices and an occasional outcropping of roots to serve as holds for hands and feet; and although the ascent was somewhat exposed, I was free from vertigo like the rest of our family. After something of a struggle, I reached the top in triumph, enjoying thoroughly the elation of a successful climb, and only regretting I had not carried with me a flag to hoist and thus to claim possession of a small, charming and hitherto unknown kingdom. The centre of the flat top supplied what appeared to be a natural stone table, and this table was even conveniently surrounded by lower flat moss-covered stones. It looked to me as if the good spirits of the mountain had prepared this small area for the enjoyment of a family.

It seemed a good idea to share my new kingdom with princes and princesses, and so I descended to the others and began showing them the grips and holds until, after mutual help, we were all on top in a new and exciting playground. We spent many hours there from then on. There was even a natural little cave in which we could store freshly picked hazelnuts and other fruits of the local earth.

We gave several banquets on the rock, serving our guests with berries, nuts and fruit which older dinner guests tactfully enjoyed. Father's closest friend, Professor Koenigstein, was an honoured guest on our rock-top eyrie. He was already in his late fifties, but he swept up the rocks as quickly as a squirrel without waiting for instructions. As a matter of fact, he had just returned from a rock-climbing holiday in the Dolomites and was, in consequence, still in training.

The last social event was disappointing. It was late in the season when we decided to give a grand evening banquet, a good time for nuts and berries, but the timing of the banquet meant that the younger children would have to leave early. Our choice of guests had become limited, but the cook, the chambermaid and the baker's boy, the young fellow who had played the guitar during the *Alm* expedition, accepted our invitation. We worked hard to supply extra large helpings of hazelnuts and blackberries and, when we had attempted some decoration with Chinese lanterns, the rock-top was ready and the hosts and hostesses eagerly awaiting the arrival of the guests.

There was a little difficulty in arranging the ascent of the chambermaid, and more in hoisting up the cook, but by applying the alpine plan of flour-bag technique, two pushing behind and two hauling from above, the ladies arrived safely in the banqueting place. As for the baker's boy, an experienced mountaineer who liked to show off, he practically walked up the side of the rock whistling with his hands in his pockets.

The party did not develop in the way I had expected. The younger children had soon to go, and my well-prepared role of host was quickly played out. I found it impossible to persuade the cook, the chambermaid and the baker's boy to show serious interest in decent games nor did they seem able to maintain a polite conversation. Eventually I became what amounted to an invisible boy, not the king of the rock-top, not even a host offering attractive and desirable refreshment in the way of hazelnuts and blackberries.

The truth is that the baker's boy became heavily preoccupied with the chambermaid, a luscious Viennese blonde who, to him, was much more diverting and stimulating than hazelnuts and my polite gossip. Soon the baker's boy had his guitar on his knee and his eyes on the curly golden locks of the chambermaid with only cursory glances at the cook, now reduced, away from her kitchen kingdom, to the role of second fiddle. He thumbed out and sang Bavarian folk-songs, the kind of songs one never sees in a *Liederbuch,* because song publishers in Bavaria do not like Bavarian prisons,which are not comfortable. At the time, I could not follow the meaning of the words, but I knew instinctively that they were very, very naughty. The evening ended for me in sadness and for the cook and chambermaid in much giggling and blushing.

I might mention here that I heard the same folk-songs years later. In 1915, as a sergeant in the Austrian Horse Artillery, I had crawled out from the dug-out at the end of a severe Russian winter to begin cutting my long beard with the only pair of scissors available. Sergeants in the Horse Artillery of any country are closely akin in not being easily shocked, and I was no exception. I was glad to hear my men singing those songs, because it meant they were happy again.

But I still recall my sadness that night at the end of the top-of-the-rock hazelnut and blackberry banquet. I had always thought that baker's boy a nice boy and a good friend. I did not think him a nice boy any more, and he was no longer my friend. He had ruined my party; he had not respected me as his host, and he had not taken his share of the hazelnuts.

We were all sitting one evening outside the villa with the baker and his family when the subject of my rock came up. The baker remarked quite proudly that when he had first seen us children playing on it, he had at once written to the forest authorities for an official permit which would legalize our doing so. He explained that these isolated rock outcroppings were under special protection. Permission had been granted for the current season.

I was thunderstruck. I owned that rock by right of conquest since, I believed, I was the first human being to set foot on its top; and now I was being told that I was only tolerated in my kingdom as one of the children of an esteemed visitor whom the authorities wanted to oblige. My pride was grievously assaulted. My title to my kingdom on the rock was not based on conquest but on a mere document, probably adorned with a fifty-pfennig stamp, issued by the Royal Bavarian Forestry Commission.

We Freud boys followed the example of all city visitors on holiday in the Bavarian mountains and wore the leather shorts and the costume that goes with them. This makes a holiday in the Bavarian and Austrian mountains unique, because it is not usual in other parts of the world for visitors to copy what amounts to peasant dress. Mother, incidentally, was always rather parsimonious in everything that did not concern father. This had been a grim necessity in her younger days, an attitude of mind towards spending money which had become second nature even when father became much better off. This was reflected in our leather shorts which, by the way, are expensive when cut from real staghide. Even the cheaper ones, cut from chamois leather, were five times as dear as shorts made from cloth. Buying leather shorts for three growing boys therefore demanded great prudence from mother. She could easily admit the lasting qualities of leather shorts and feel some comfort in the knowledge that men and boys actually prefer well-worn and shabby ones as a badge of local prestige and experience; but in the case of growing boys, the shorts would not have time to reach this desirable condition if bought to fit. There is an old photograph of my two brothers and myself in alpine costume when we were about nine, eight and seven years old respectively. The hems of our shorts, it will be observed, cover nearly the whole of our knees. In contrast, there is another photograph of myself at about fifteen, with the shorts covering only half my thigh, which was much more comfortable. The reason for this divergence in purely family fashion is perhaps obvious. The shorts I wore in the photograph with my brothers are the same shorts, or most probably so, that I wore at fifteen. Mother always bought shorts a few sizes too big so that we should not outgrow them too soon.

The preference for leather shorts with a well-worn look, not shiny and immaculate, extended even to the Emperor, it was said. He was often photographed in the country in alpine costume, and His Majesty's leather shorts always appeared to be well-used. It was rumoured that his valet broke them in before they were allowed to adorn the Imperial thighs. It was the general opinion that if one wore new leather shorts, one might be mistaken for a member of the Bauern Kapelle, the peasants' brass band; but it is unlikely that the Emperor Franz Josef had any fears on this score.

There are slight differences in the alpine costumes worn in the various alpine valleys, but since my experience is limited to Aussee and Berchtesgaden I can only discuss them. I would say that the latter are much gayer. The Berchtesgaden man wears bows of green silk, while the Styrian peasant is content to show stag-horn buttons. Both have chamois embroidered on the leather, but while the Austrian beast looks serene and quiet, the Bavarian animal seems gay, laughing and even a little bit drunk.

Mother had a much easier and less expensive job dressing her three daughters in alpine costume during the holidays. They wore the dirndl which is, as most people know, a simply cut one-piece frock of flowered cotton with a square-cut *décolleté*, and controlled by a belt. A shawl is usually worn in addition.

We were often delighted to have proof that our dress harmonized with the scenery and the local people of Koenigsee; again and again we were mistaken for peasant children. I think we were delighted because we liked the place and its good-natured, gay and friendly people who, while always polite and obliging, were never subservient. There was, too, the fun of dressing up in a highly attractive uniform.

While I have been reliving these happy memories, my sister Mathilde has recalled with amusement an adventure she enjoyed one day when she was loitering, in her usual holiday dirndl, near the Seelaende, the boat-jetty at Koenigsee. Some weeks of sunny weather had bronzed Mathilde almost to blackness. She was somewhat startled when a Prussian lady emerged from a crowd of excursionists to lick her finger and then to press this firmly on the back of Mathilde's neck.

"What on earth are you doing, Theodora?" shouted her husband, a tall monocled man with a "Kaiser Wilhelm" moustache, in his shrill and unpleasantly penetrating Prussian tone.

"Oh, it's all right, Justinian!" cried the lady; "I was only trying to find out whether or not the colour would come off."

# CHAPTER X

ALTHOUGH father had much to do during our summers at Koenigsee, writing for hours at a time, he occasionally put aside his work and took the whole family for an excursion. There was one place he liked best; and this was the small peninsula of St Bartholomae near the southerly end of the lake, a truly lovely spot where wild grandeur was given humanity by a very old inn and an equally old, if not older, chapel or church. This was probably the most often photographed and most often painted spot in Germany, if not in Europe.

Here the steep eastern flank of the Watzman formed a rock wall reaching to upwards of 7,000 feet and, seen from the lake, it was easy to imagine that a stone dropped from its summit would land on the roof of the church, although, in fact, a grove stretched between the church and the base of the rock wall, where a miniature glacier passed from the steep rocks to the level of the lake shore. I may say that later in the century, this Watzman East Wand Flank became enormously popular with leading German rock-climbers. Several lives were lost here.

This rock wall offers one of the longest climbs in the Eastern Alps. It could not then be done in one day, the climber having to carry with him bivouac equipment to permit him to spend a cold night half-way up on a few square feet of partially exposed rock, securing his bivouac with ropes attached to steel rings hammered into crevices.

In the last few years mountaineers from Munich have built a tiny shelter, a corrugated-iron box, into the last third of the eastern flank to provide shelter for climbers in need. When we stayed in Koenigsee the rock wall had already been conquered, but apart from a small circle of prominent climbers, nobody knew much about it.

Although the peninsula of St Bartholomae offered much to father and us children, I think the journey there and back gave more in the way of interest and entertainment. We occasionally used one of the large flat boats, a kind of water omnibus, rowed by four strong local women and steered by a man. This boat was always crowded with tourists, who sat in their places under the strictest discipline, never being allowed to stand up nor to change places—a necessary rule, because, unaware of the slightest danger, these tourists would have moved about for the least important of reasons and capsized the boat. Thus the story Uncle Gustave in the bow wanted to tell Uncle Karl in the stern had to wait until we landed; and Aunt Olga, who, from her position in the barge could not see the tiny waterfall enjoyed by others, had to be content with a description and to resist any desire to stand up.

The big moment in the journey was the echo-shooting and to this we always looked forward. At a moment when the boat was making her slow way past the highest and steepest rocky walls, the steersman, a fine specimen of steel-muscled manhood, doubtless a poacher in his spare time, would take from a sack an ancient heavy pistol—a terrifying and awe-inspiring instrument I recognized as of the kind used by Germans in the Thirty Years' War. But in case I may appear at this stage of my life to be a prodigy of historical knowledge, I had better explain that we had all been taken recently to our beloved Burgtheatre in Vienna to see a performance of Schiller's *Wallenstein* set in the period of the Thirty Years' War. The soldiers of the play used these flint-lock pistols, papier mâché and wood, doubtless, since the real thing as used by the skipper of the Koenigsee barge was largely of iron and so heavy that only a strong man might lift it with one hand. I found it interesting to build up a long story, tracing the history of the skipper's ancient pistol down through the centuries, in which marauding Swedish horsemen played a prominent, if not distinguished, part: but the story, apart from being long, is adorned with so much complication that I doubt if any one would enjoy it as much as I did.

In the meantime, the skipper, well aware of the mounting tension he was creating amongst his passengers, and with one eye on his steering, proceeded calmly to load his weapon until, in good time, he raised it above his head. After a pause long enough to stretch the tension to almost unbearable tautness, during which three of the boatwomen put their calloused hands to their ears (the fourth lady was stone-deaf), he fired: and at once the sound of the explosion reverberated, echoed and re-echoed from mountain wall to mountain wall in a highly dramatic and impressive way, increasing in sound, decreasing to mere whispers of distant echoes and finally sleeping in dream echoes. With kindly smiles, the boatwomen took up their oars and the journey proceeded under the command of the skipper, whose bombardment of that imprisoned air seemed to have won him added respect.

Father was very fond of St Bartholomae. The place had the happiest effect on him, allowing him to abandon his usual reserve and even to become a little playful. I recall one day when we were disembarking in that usual hurry which invariably controls landing excursionists. A Prussian lady immediately in front of father became an unconscious menace by tucking her sharp-pointed umbrella under her arm with the point facing backwards, thus gravely threatening the eyes of those who followed her. Without hesitation, father drew the umbrella back from under her arm, quickly turned it and with a disarming smile and bow handed it back. No words were exchanged. The lady was somewhat astonished but not vexed, and I think a lesson may have been taken to heart.

Once landed on the peninsula, there was much to amuse us. Strawberries were plentiful in the grove behind the old church and, I think owing to the shelter given by the great rock wall, the berries were larger than those found anywhere else. We spent hours with father picking strawberries. Then we could play on the small glacier, rather dirty in appearance at this end of its journey. It was called Eiskapelle, the ice chapel. In the strictest sense of the word the Eiskapelle is not a glacier, but father explained to us carefully how glaciers are formed, how they flow in effect like a river although their movement is imperceptible. He said we might drink the melted ice from the glacier provided we added a few drops of lemon juice to the very cold water, and he took from his pocket a small bottle of lemon juice to demonstrate. People, not even doctors, do not make a habit of carrying small bottles of lemon juice in their pockets, and so I imagine father had come prepared for this little lecture.

The old inn had a charming garden shaded by old trees, with the usual outdoor tables for guests, who were attended by girls clad in a rather theatrical form of the local dirndl. The entrance hall of the inn was decorated with numbers of old pictures of the large fish caught in the lake throughout the centuries. These are salmon-trout, called *Saiblings* locally. They have the shape and speckles of ordinary trout, but the flesh is like salmon if of a paler pink shade. They are quite delicious to eat. It was suspected that the innkeeper thought guests rather tactless if they compared the fish on their plates with the fish in the pictures, the comparison making the latter somewhat gigantic if not fabulous *Saiblings*.

No one was permitted to stay overnight at St Bartholomae, but whether or not this rule applied to the innkeeper and his staff I cannot say. Someone in addition to the ghosts of painted, gigantic *Saiblings* was needed to guard the place when darkness fell.

An old man with a long beard and much longer telescope sat in the *Biergarten* and, by paying him twenty pfennigs, one might enjoy a peep at the chamois roaming on the slopes of the mountains. He did a brisk trade with German tourists from the lowlands but, at this time of my life, I regarded all kinds of side-shows with deep suspicion, and I never felt tempted to spend so much money on what I felt sure was a swindle. As a boy from Vienna who had had some experience of twenty-pfennig side-shows, from calves with two heads to ladies without abdomens, I looked on all such as swindles. I did not believe the old man with the long beard could focus his old telescope on real live chamois, and I darkly suspected him of planting a stuffed beast at a suitable point on the mountains. And, of course, father had taken us high enough in the mountains to see plenty of chamois, and marmots as well, without paying a pfennig. I conceded grudgingly that perhaps the old man with the long beard and his telescope supplied a need to those German trippers whose experience of this kind of animal had been limited to the sight of a neighbour's nanny-goat.

When later I had more experience with father on the higher mountains, I saw my distrust of the old man with the telescope as something rather unworthy. Apart from being a tough job to carry it so high up a mountain, a stuffed beast would not long survive alpine storms, even if birds of prey did not make short work of it; and the real chamois would not welcome in their midst a silent and motionless guest most probably smelling strongly of moth-balls.

St Bartholomae is the home of superlatives. They have there the most tasty salmon-trout, the biggest and best strawberries in the world and, a particularly proud boast, the most delicious drinking-water in the universe. This water, beautifully cool, flows strongly from a spring near the inn entrance, and although water-drinking is not normally fashionable in Bavaria, the waters of St Bartholomae are an exception because of their great fame.

There was a curious incident, commonplace enough in itself, which occurred when we were sitting in the *Biergarten* and which became impressed on my mind because of its effect on my father. Next to us sat a middle-class Berlin family including a boy of about our age. The parents sent this boy to the well with a tray carrying three empty glasses which they wanted filled. The boy's performance was not distinguished. He began by allowing the full jet of water to flow down between his shirt and his trousers which, naturally, made him shiver with cold. Eventually, he succeeded in filling the glasses to their brims and began making an uncertain progress back to his parents' table around and between other crowded tables. Because his clothing was so wet, he slipped once or twice. The first slip sent one of the glasses to the ground, where it broke, but the second slip was more serious, happening when he was trying to avoid the broken glass: the contents of the two surviving glasses went splashing into the steaming pea-soup of an indignant guest. He eventually reached his parents with the tray and the two empty glasses, but he showed no contrition; he seemed rather proud in having survived with something, even if it were only two empty glasses.

Father had at first watched this expedition with amused curiosity and, indeed, one could imagine a similar performance bringing the house down if performed by a clown at a circus; but when the boy was safely back with his parents, father remarked in a cold voice, loud enough to be heard by the parents, that he hoped none of us would give so shocking a display if sent on a similar errand. For a moment I was alarmed, fearing that he would ask one of us, probably me, to go and fetch six glasses of water; but my fears were groundless. We had plenty of water on our table and, in any case, he would have thought a model expedition by me somewhat ostentatious. The incident remains impressed on my mind because of the irritation shown by father over so unimportant an event. Later, when I was much older, I recalled the scene and began asking myself why he had been so cross. The boy who had disgraced himself so much in father's eyes was plainly Jewish in an unmistakable and not attractive way, rather like a caricature of a Jewish boy; and this was quickly seen by the Gentiles in the *Biergarten* who watched the performance with amused disdain. Perhaps father had some underlying fear that his own Jewish children would meet one day with similar treatment, deserved in this case, he thought, by a display that showed bad upbringing, that in effect let our side down. This is merely the thought that occurred to me, and it could be false. Anyway, it is futile to raise questions which cannot be answered.

We, father's Jewish children, were never conscious of anything approaching discrimination against us because of our race. Although we were not easily recognized as Jewish, we could not be mistaken for Bavarian or Austrian Gentiles. "Your children, Frau Professor," a polite German lady once remarked to mother, "look so Italian."

## CHAPTER XI

I DO not want to give the impression that the life of Sigmund Freud's children was one of uninterrupted happiness amongst *Alpenrosen,* strawberries and chamois. The summer holidays as we grew older became shorter: what had been months became weeks. However, I think most older people will agree when they review their youth that the holidays are the western mountain-tops upon which the sun's glow remains longest, long after the plains of workaday life are hidden in shadows or darkness.

Our parents had arranged to send my brother Oliver and myself to an old-fashioned kind of grammar school, the "Humanistic Gymnasium", where pupils were trained for a career in medicine and law. The youngest brother was sent to the more modern *Realschule* to be prepared for the Technical High School. At both schools certain times were reserved for visits from parents, who might interview the teachers regarding the progress, or otherwise, of their children.

Mother was most conscientious about this, and I was not unaware of the effects of these visits. Reports gained about Oliver's progress saw her happy and satisfied, but the interviews with my teachers had a depressing effect and went on having this effect until my last year. Until then, I was not a satisfactory pupil, just managing to squeeze near the bottom of my class without suffering the dreaded *Nachpruefung,* an examination set in the autumn for doubtful pupils to decide whether or not they should pass to a higher class. A failure, which I avoided by the skin of my teeth, would have ruined the whole following summer for me.

Happily, the last year of my studies showed a dramatic change. From the bottom I rose to the top, passing the *Reifepruefung* (matriculation) with the highest honours. This transformation was quite inexplicable to my parents and, strangely enough, equally so to me.

Mother was nothing if not thorough and when she visited my

school she neglected none of my teachers, not even the *Turn-lehrer,* the gymnastic teacher, who had few callers and appreciated this attention, translating it into special attention to me. In addition, I had got hold of a pamphlet on physical development which proved most useful. I do know that these widely advertised books and pamphlets offering readers detailed instructions about physical development are often ridiculed, but I followed the instructions in my book with the happiest results. I had now been given a room of my own in the Bergasse flat and every evening I exercised with great enthusiasm, spending hours slowly strengthening my weak and undeveloped body—up and down from the floor on my finger tips, deep breathing, jumping and bending my body about until I was completely exhausted.

This worked so well that the day came when I felt I might challenge those of my class-mates who, owing to my physical weakness, had felt safe in beating and insulting me. The result was a series of duels, boxing in fact, fought on a nearby enclosed space. These events drew a lot of spectators eager to see the defeat of a weakling, but they soon lost interest, for my opponents were knocked out rather mercilessly and soon decided to leave me in peace. The last of my former tormentors refused to accept the challenge and he had to be dealt with in the intervals between lessons. And thus I gained the reputation of a bully and a ruffian—undeserved, I felt: my conscience was clear since I felt I was attempting nothing more than retrospective self-defence.

Most of our lessons in those days in Vienna were extremely dull and I cannot believe that the teachers were less bored than the pupils: the former a mixed bag, some clever and malicious, others kindly buffoons. After the matriculation the traditional banquet was given to the teachers by the pupils, but ours ended badly, in discord, rudeness and mutual recriminations.

I think the committee in charge of the banquet arrangements were really to blame. Under the influence of a few sons of wealthy parents, they made the mistake of supplying more wine than was necessary and of a quality much better and more potent than the majority of the teachers and pupils were used to. Some of the teachers were sufficiently ill-advised to take this chance of diffusing political propaganda, on behalf of National-German ideas, hoping to influence young people, some of whom might now step out into public life. There were odd clashes, and it was only with difficulty that I was prevented from challenging the leading propagandist to a duel. My class-mates who held me back explained that I could have no right to make such a challenge until I had been properly inscribed as a university student.

It is usual for old students of such grammar schools to have reunions at intervals, but in our case wars and political upheavals prevented such. In consequence, with the exception of a few who won fame, I have no idea what happened to the majority of my old class-mates. Erich Kleiber, the celebrated German conductor, was one of the exceptions. He was a pleasant kind-hearted boy, popular with both teachers and pupils. I recall a day when the *Katechet*, the Roman Catholic priest responsible for religious instruction of the Gentiles in our class, came into the room to arrange an excursion into the Wienerwald, always a welcome and bright interval in the dreary school life of those days. Kleiber, himself a Catholic and on most cordial terms with the priest, threw himself into his arms—not an easy feat, because the priest was a big man and Kleiber very small—and begged him to take the Jewish boys too on the excursion, something which could not be done.

The educational scheme of our school included open-air games with concentration on soccer; but in our case there was no useful organization. No one worried about football kit and so there were no distinguishing colours that could be trusted. The goals were marked by heaps of coats, but what made these games so very difficult to play was the absence of a referee, made worse by the fact that only one boy knew the rules, or said he did: the result being that his side was invariably right when an argument began and the other side quite wrong. Finding all this arguing and cheating obnoxious, I kept away from the soccer games as much as possible; but I do not think I was missed: I was an indifferent player.

Queerly enough, this boy who knew all the rules and posed as an expert at soccer was, like the late Erich Kleiber, one of the exceptions amongst my class-mates: I learnt of his fate. He became very rich during the inflation and, like many another, he collapsed with that house of cards. Scraping together all the money he could lay hands on, he bought the most fashionable *sports-cabriolet* available on the automobile market and sent this as a gift to a charming and very beautiful cabaret singer. After that, without waiting for an acknowledgement of the gift or a gesture of thanks from the beautiful girl, he went home and shot himself.

# CHAPTER XII

FATHER hated bicycles: I don't really know why, but dislike them he did even though friends like old Professor Kassowitz were enthusiastic cyclists; Professor Kassowitz often took his whole family on long two-wheel excursions. The heirs of these enthusiasts are the lithe young fellows and even girls on bicycles one sees today in big cities floating so swiftly along as they juggle with death amidst the motor traffic. In those days, motor-cars were still rare; and the bicycle, which could defeat distance and time, had the quality almost of magic, leaving the horse, whether ridden or driven, far behind. Roads were not what they are now and adventurous cyclists had many troubles (and many bumps) as they made their way, but the craze was a real one and, to father's mind, afflicted all classes. Motor-cycles soon appeared to win father's detestation. However, father's dislike of bicycles did not extend to forbidding his children to indulge in the new sport and we were all equipped with good new models. This did not prevent him from expressing his feelings whenever he had the chance.

I remember the time when father made a reconnaissance tour to find a new holiday resort for the family. The place he was considering was Mondsee in the Salzkammergut. From here he sent home a poem condemning Mondsee as unsuitable, the burden of the verse being the great number of cyclists on the main road there, making it quite unsafe for children. Father's verse does not lend itself to translation chiefly because of the delightful acrobatics with the German language he appeared to enjoy. This verse said in effect that one had to hate cyclists because of the dust they raised and the number of children they knocked down. (Weil sie den Staub linieren und die Kinder ueberfuehren.)

His emphasis on the knocking down of children was perhaps unfortunate since it was not long before his eldest son knocked down a child and found himself arrested and marched to the nearest police station.

I was cycling home with a class-mate from a game of soccer, the usual mad kind of contest mixed up with quarrels and fierce arguments which, as we rode, I dismissed from my mind in favour of the story of Achilles and Hector which we had been reading in school that day. We had reached the part where Achilles had slain Hector and was dragging the corpse of the latter around the walls of Troy. My imagination had always been fertile and in those days it was particularly lush, permitting my mind to dwell on all the gory details, and allowing me to see myself sometimes as the dead Hector, sometimes as the triumphant Achilles, with a natural preference for the part of Achilles. Suddenly—I was at that moment Achilles—the chariot turned over and I found myself lying on Hector's imaginary corpse which, however, began wriggling as it emitted an evil smell, assuming reality in the body of a small boy, an unclean bundle of rags, while my bicycle lay on its side near by. Happily, neither the boy nor I had suffered material damage and the bicycle was all right.

I think the boy would have liked to run away when we had got to our feet, but we had become surrounded by a hostile crowd, the scum of the Prater, unlikely to show anything but sympathy for a small member of their own class.

A policeman appeared and marched me with my bicycle to the nearby police station. The victim, most unwillingly, was forced to march with us, showing his distaste by whimpering. My class-mate followed; but the hostile crowd paused on the street, not one of its members having any desire voluntarily to enter a police station.

We had not long to wait before the police officer on duty began the investigation by questioning me. Since I had no idea how the accident had occurred, everything having happened so quickly, I showed considerable hesitation in my replies, which, however, carefully avoided any reference to Achilles in his chariot. Fortunately, my class-mate clarified the situation by telling the officer that he had witnessed the whole event and would be glad to offer evidence. Permission being granted, the officer (and I, incidentally) learnt that the small boy had dashed into the street from behind a stationary coal van and had charged into me on the bicycle, bringing us all to the ground. Although I could not remember the collision, it sounded plausible and I am sure it was the truth.

"Why," demanded the police officer, turning to the victim and not speaking in a very kindly way, "why don't you look where you are going?" The question was unanswerable then as it has become equally unanswerable a thousand times a week in most great cities today; and so the small boy could think of nothing better to do than to exchange his whimpering for loud and penetrating howling. The police officer gave orders that he should be examined next day by a police surgeon, something that increased the terror of the boy, and, turning towards me in a friendly manner, he asked for my name and address, and said I might go.

The result of all this was that I got home very late, after my brothers and sisters had gone to bed, but I had an interested audience in father and mother. In my story I pointed out repeatedly how very helpful and even friendly the police officer had been, something which mother, who had asked many questions, fully appreciated. Father, on the other hand, who had listened in silence, finally closed the meeting by remarking somewhat coldly, "Without doubt, that police officer is a cyclist himself."

What Ernest Jones in his biography of my father calls "the emergence from isolation" did not make a welcome change to us. I think we preferred father's isolation. Father was not only generous with his money, he was also generous with his time, although, in all conscience, he had not much of the latter to give. He worked ten hours a day on practising analysis, apart from his writing and correspondence.

The children's contacts with the learned men who came to see him to discuss his theories were naturally of the slightest. Such visitors were usually asked to stay for a meal and nearly always, we saw, they had little interest in the food they were offered and perhaps less in mother and us children. However, they always worked hard to maintain a polite conversation with their hostess and her children, most often about the theatre or sport, the weather not being a useful stand-by as it is in England on these occasions. Nevertheless, it could be seen quite easily that all they wanted was to get this social occasion over and done with and to retreat with father to his study to hear more about psychoanalysis. Jung was an exception. He never made the slightest attempt to make polite conversation with mother or us children but pursued the debate which had been interrupted by the call to dinner. Jung on these occasions did all the talking and father with unconcealed delight did all the listening. There was little we could understand, but I know I found, as did father, his way of outlining a case most fascinating. I can recall today the case of a man who, after being shy and inhibited during the first two-thirds of his life, developed in late middle age a forceful and dominating personality, and the story of another man, a schizophrenic, whose drawing showed an amazing vitality and excellence.

Neither cases had in themselves much importance. Discussed by Jung, they became clear pictures.

Those of my readers who have studied modern psychology have learned much about Jung—probably as much as about Freud—but to others his name may mean nothing. Jung held a leading position in Switzerland's most famous psychiatric clinic and he was a scientist of high reputation. I think his most outstanding characteristics were his vitality, his liveliness, his ability to project his personality and to control those who listened to him.

Jung had a commanding presence. He was very tall and broad-shouldered, holding himself more like a soldier than a man of science and medicine. His head was purely Teutonic with a strong chin, a small moustache, blue eyes and thin close-cropped hair. I met Jung only once. When, later in life, I moved much in psychoanalytical circles, he had already left the Freud-adherents; I cannot flatter myself that he ever noticed me.

Sister Mathilde told me that one day when she was shopping in Vienna with Jung and his family, soldiers lining the street were ordered to attention. The Emperor was about to pass. With a quick "Excuse me, please!" Jung ran to join the crowd as enthusiastic as any boy.

One of the very few psychoanalysts who showed interest in his host's children at the Bergasse was Dr Sandor Ferenczy of Budapest. He was high in father's favour. A lively, witty and most affectionate man, he found not the slightest difficulty in winning my devoted friendship, a friendship not affected by the fact that I knew he was assuming the role of a mentor in a worthy desire to help me on my way through adolescence to manhood.

I never met Dr Adler, so often associated with my father's name by biographers and those who write about psychoanalysis.

We were aware of the Wednesday night meetings in the waiting-room of the Bergasse flat, where great minds, led by father, strove to bring to the surface knowledge long suspected but still fugitive and still unrecorded with that precision science demands. We heard people arriving, but we seldom saw them. The inevitable curiosity of a boy allowed me to inspect the arrangements in the waiting-room before the guests arrived. Near each chair on the table there was always an ashtray from father's collection, some of them of Chinese jade. I saw the necessity for this multiplicity of ashtrays one night when, on returning from a dance, I looked into the waiting-room from which the guests had only just withdrawn. The room was still thick with smoke and it seemed to me a wonder that human beings had been able to live in it for hours, let alone to speak in it without choking. I could never understand how father could endure it, let alone enjoy it: which he did. It is possible that to some of his guests the smoke-charged atmosphere was an ordeal, but it is certain they thought the price low in exchange for the high privilege of a close personal contact with a great teacher.

It was very seldom that I met Dr Fliess, father's best friend for sixteen years, and I cannot recall any personal details about him. His portrait, even after the ending of this great friendship, always remained in father's study in a place of honour. Another friendship, that with Dr Breuer, had ended long before my years of consciousness; but relations with Dr Breuer's family remained most cordial and I still have a few pictures showing a mixed bag of Freud children and the grandchildren of Josef Breuer playing in summer holiday mood in Altaussee. By a strange coincidence a grandson of Josef Breuer and a grandson of Sigmund Freud (my son, in fact), both British officers in No. 1 Special Force, parachute-jumped from the same aeroplane into enemy territory during the last months of the war, and both survived.

# CHAPTER XIII

THE holiday plans followed by the family in 1906 were quite ambitious. We went farther from Vienna than we had ever been before, twice as far in fact, to a mountain resort in the most southerly part of the Tyrol, close to the Italian border. It was Lavarone in the Valsugana. Possibly we were the first Viennese family ever to visit Lavarone for a summer holiday. Sister Mathilde has explained to me why father chose this place, a story I think a little sentimental and not to my taste; but because it is true, there is no harm in telling it now.

A friend of Uncle Alexander, Jewish and from Moravia, and about father's age, was a gifted poet but not successful in a pecuniary sense; indeed, he did not earn enough to ensure a decent living. Father took Mathilde with him to call on this gentleman in his modest quarters when he was seriously ill, dying, in fact. I might remark here that on such occasions father carried with him more than good wishes for a speedy recovery.

During the course of their conversation, the dying poet exclaimed, "Oh, if I could only see the laburnum blossoming once more in Lavarone!"

"Where," father asked, "is Lavarone?" And at once the poet began a description which must have been touching, since sister Mathilde has never forgotten it. The place was 3,800 feet up in the highlands and in consequence the spring flowers were only beginning to bloom there when summer had come to the valleys. The sick man recommended the Hotel du Lac where he had stayed and enjoyed himself.

Later, months later, perhaps even a year or two later—Mathilde cannot be sure—father was touring in the South Tyrol and found himself not far from Lavarone. He evidently recalled the dying poet's recommendation and decided to look at the place. He wrote home describing the wonderful fir forests and the restful air of loneliness which attracted him and, doubtless, he made arrangements with the landlord of the Hotel du Lac. In due course, we found ourselves there.

The rural population in the surrounding country as well as the shopkeepers, the hotelkeepers and the clergy of Lavarone were of Italian stock; but although there were then rumours of a possible war between Austria and Italy, the Austrian authorities treated the Italians quite fairly with not a hint of oppression, and there were no serious signs of any friction between the differing nationalities. There was, however, one rather amusing incident which failed to disturb the prevailing serenity: when patriotic Austrians wanted to bind garlands to celebrate the Emperor's birthday, all the local shops suddenly found themselves out of stock of both string and wire.

The Hotel du Lac, which perhaps obviously took its name from an adjacent small green mountain lake, was most comfortable. The lake was rather smaller than the Thumsee lake but we had it very much to ourselves except for visits from an Austrian detachment of soldiers stationed near by. There were one or two rowing-boats and we could do a little fishing, but we spent more time swimming, although the water was pretty cold owing to the lake's high altitude. We found a good spot for swimming where some bushes on the shore gave privacy for undressing, although not quite enough for some with emphasized modesty. For these shy undressers we erected a kind of cabin with sticks and a length of canvas; but we were often defeated by the habit this cabin had of disintegrating at the moment when the undresser, nearly always a female, was pulling her last garment over her head.

This happened one day to one of our visitors, a very fat lady from Vienna, when the shelter collapsed around her so suddenly that I, standing near in my ill-fitting swim-suit, had not time to look the other way. Free of her stays and the other necessary furniture which normally contained her bulk, she looked like an outsize jelly-fish; but although, naturally, I was much too polite to remark on this, the shock her appearance gave me must have been expressed clearly in my startled eyes, sufficiently clearly, I think, to inspire retaliation. Quickly reorganizing her flowing-away kind of figure inside our best and biggest towel, she looked me up and down and remarked, "Boy, you look like a paper-knife."

A few hundred yards away from us, the Austrian infantry bathed in the suits they had worn for their medical examinations; but the soldiers and civilians did not mix on these occasions.

At Lavarone, I was at the age when most boys keep diaries, and by a lucky chance, the diary I kept there has survived with the few papers I managed to carry to London as a refugee after escaping from the Nazis. Like all such, its style is cryptic and the information it offers is not important to any one but myself; but it does allow me to recall clearly the events we enjoyed during a few weeks of the first summer holiday at Lavarone in 1906. My walking tour with father to the Lake of Molveno is carefully recorded as well as the fact that father took the children daily to swim in the lake, bald facts written carefully so long ago, but which bring back the great amount of sunshine we enjoyed that year when, after the frigidity of the water, we could lie on the rough grass of the meadow in the warm sunshine at our swimming place. My swimming improved enormously until I could even carry my small sister Anna on my back. There were long walks with father through the beautiful forests, sometimes with all three boys; and on one great occasion when I alone went with father, we stayed away thirteen hours, having only one rest and finding a lot of edelweiss, evidence that we had reached a fair height up the mountains.

During these excursions, we often had to cross the frontier into Italy, something which at that time required no formalities and certainly no passports, only a little difficulty in changing money when we bought simple provisions—bread, wine, cheese and salami—in the small shops called *generi misti,* mixed goods.

My diary recalls that one day Ernst, my brother, caught a "real" fish, which I assume means an edible fish of respectable size as opposed to what we usually caught which were useless for eating. We caught plenty of crayfish, but I do not record that we handed these in to the hotel kitchen to supplement the menu, something which was quite unnecessary, because the food at the Hotel du Lac was exquisite in quality and in great variety. Always at dinner there were a number of courses, including fish, poultry and meat, most luxurious when compared with what is offered these days even at great cost; but in those days, before the First World War, no hotel could long survive or maintain a reputation if it did not offer a first-rate menu.

The landlord's son boasted to me that he had been in London, in Paris, in Naples and even Egypt, to say nothing of other places.

To a boy like myself who had seen little of the outer world, this was impressive, but my respect diminished somewhat when he explained that he had worked for his living in these places, sometimes as a waiter, occasionally as a cook and once as a secretary. I had yet to learn what I could not then understand: this practice of working one's way and picking up languages is the only way to make of oneself a really good hotelkeeper.

We spent two consecutive summers at Lavarone and father and we children made many good friends, especially with a charming and well-educated man and his family from Padova. There were three girls and one boy, rather younger than we were as a family; but we played together happily. I promptly fell in love with one of the girls, with Titian hair and lively manners; but while this had much beauty and wonder for me, it was accepted by the others as a commonplace and caused no surprise whatever.

These people came to the hotel some time after our arrival and the father of the family, who was a manufacturer of small useful articles connected with the boot trade, had the title of *cavaliere*. Having introduced himself to father, giving his name and title, he remarked, "Noi siamo Ebrei (We are Jews)." Father said, in effect, "So are we." This may seem an unusual way of introducing oneself, but as I then thought, and still think, it is a practical proceeding which allows everybody to know just where he is. Nobody, so far as I know, can distinguish an Italian Jew from an Italian Gentile from facial characteristics. Perhaps the Jew may look a little more Italian.

On clear cool evenings, father and the *cavaliere* from Padova used to walk up and down in the small park at the back of the hotel deep in conversation. Both men spoke Italian and German but during these walks they used German. One night when they were promenading I placed myself near by, hålf hidden under a large fir-tree, deeply interested, apparently, in studying the movements of a stag beetle who seemed undecided whether to go up or to go down the tree-trunk. In fact, I wanted to hear what father was saying, hoping he might be discussing dreams. He was, in fact, explaining newly discovered scientific theories, but not dreams: he was outlining the "period theory" of his former friend, Dr Fliess.

I was not the only one in the family to find himself concerned with romance during this holiday. Sister Mathilde was also embroiled: as harmlessly but, in her case, a somewhat more adult affair.

It happened that Mathilde was walking alone one day, something she loved to do, when, on a road through the forest, she saw a platoon of infantry approaching. She was pleasantly surprised when the young officer smartly called his men to attention and ordered eyes right as they passed. This impressive military salute, so well carried out, startled and delighted Mathilde, who was unaware that the officer had flown in the teeth of Austrian army regulations; but I expect he felt that rules applicable to Vienna or Salzburg might be forgotten in a mountain forest when one meets a pretty girl.

She met the officer later and he began at once to court her, explaining that he had heard about the professor and his family staying at the Hotel du Lac. He said that he wanted to pay his respects to compatriots who spoke his own language since he felt lonely and isolated, the Italian population and even his own Czech men being Austrians merely because they had to be. None of his soldiers could understand German beyond the standardized words of command used throughout the polyglot Austrian army of that time.

Without doubt many of my readers will picture this young Austrian officer as a reckless dashing young fellow, up to his neck in debt, an amateur steeplechaser devoted to champagne and the prettiest ladies of the *demi-monde*. Austrian officers are nearly always pictured like that in books and films and perhaps they may have had some reality in feudal cavalry regiments. I have never met such. The truth is that the average infantry subaltern of the Austrian army then, as probably now, was of modest upbringing, often very poor and never in debt because no one would ever risk lending him money or giving him much credit. On the whole he was a simple fellow and endearing.

Mathilde's lieutenant was of this class and type, a prudent young man who would send home to his mother in her small village anything he could save from his small pay rather than spend it on an extra glass of beer.

Father invited the young officer to meals with us at the Hotel du Lac, most probably a pleasant contrast with the officer's mess.

He looked quite smart in his field uniform, as do most young Austrian officers; and it seemed to me that he was quite a hero. However, when he came to see Mathilde at our swimming place and began crawling about the shallow water in a badly fitting swim-suit, he appeared much less heroic. He could not swim.

Father showed himself charming and agreeable to this young man, listening with apparent interest when he did his best to talk in an educated kind of way. It happened that at this time another young man paid us a short visit, a young scientist from Hungary, Dr Barany, who later won the Nobel prize. I watched with interest both of these young men walking with father. They were rather alike—fair, broad-shouldered and well-built. Both were taller than father, and so both looked down on him with admiration.

I was greatly impressed by Dr Barany: he was the most powerful swimmer I had ever seen. Some pity modified my liking for the gentle lieutenant: it was indeed a great pity he could not swim a stroke.

Swimming was not, of course, the standard by which father judged people. Different as they were in education and upbringing, father treated both young men alike: with great friendliness and, perhaps, an equally great reserve.

# CHAPTER XIV

THE superb cuisine of the Hotel du Lac was most probably why a very important person chose it, rather than its more modern competitor, the Grand Hotel, for a banquet to which were invited the officers of the local garrison. The very important person was a member of the Imperial family and, in consequence, we children enjoyed the excitement of having a prince practically at home with us.

In looking back on this dinner party, I have some regret that this prince was not the Archduke Eugen whom I met twenty-five years later at a banquet given by the Union of Royalist Ex-Officers to which I then belonged: because the Archduke Eugen, besides being about a foot taller than any ordinary human being, had magnificent charm and any party honoured by his presence was bound to be a pleasing success. If I am to be really honest, I must admit that at this distance of time I am not entirely certain regarding the precise identity of the prince we saw at the Hotel du Lac, and neither my brother nor my sister can help me. I am practically certain, however, that the gentleman was Franz Ferdinand, the heir to the throne who was murdered in 1914 at Sarajevo, a crime held responsible for starting the First World War.

The great hotel dining-room had been cleared of ordinary mortals and the tables arranged in horseshoe fashion, thus allowing even the most junior officers to sit fairly close to the prince who, as an Imperial General, naturally had the place of honour.

Whenever the door opened to let the waiters and the manager in or out—and it opened frequently—we children, crouched near the door, enjoyed a full view of the proceedings. However, a particular view of the Archduke himself tended to be interrupted by the junior officers nearest the door. Nevertheless, we could see the royal fork moving up and down efficiently, something we noted as a sign of a healthy appetite. Except that he looked morose and ill-tempered, the Archduke behaved quite normally. The morose ill-temper may have been natural to him, or something may have upset him. Now and then he made a remark to one or other of the senior officers sitting near him, most probably a polite and meaningless question which did not demand from him much attention to any reply. It was rumoured that he was rather deaf.

The presence of the Archduke seemed to have a paralysing effect on the junior officers sitting not far from our observation post, and this tended to put them off their victuals, a shocking waste, we children thought, in view of the delicious food. We decided that they feared that at any moment they might be spoken to by His Imperial Highness. It would be shocking to reply to royalty with one's mouth full.

We were particularly delighted with a young ensign because he looked hardly more than a boy. He cut his meat into tiny particles and picked these up like a bird. My guess was that he wanted to be ready to reply to the Archduke if addressed. One of my sisters thought he was so excited that he was unable to swallow more than morsels; but another opinion clung to the thought that the young man, unused to urban manners, thought this was the correct way to eat when one was within a few feet of an archduke.

The proprietor's son, who had organized the banquet, went in and out, wearing his widest and brightest smile within the dining-room, but instantly exchanging this for an expression of grave concentration when the door closed behind him. We children, crouching near that door, decided that it might be safest to keep out of his way while the weight of responsibility rested so heavily on his shoulders and so we withdrew to explore the landing where the officers had left their cloaks and hats. Mathilde instantly guessed which cap belonged to the royal visitor and, very cautiously, she took it from its hook to examine it. It was lined with white silk adorned with an Imperial crown embroidered in gold. Mathilde was even bold enough to put it on her head for a few seconds, where it fitted very well. When it suddenly occurred to us that this act of *lèse-majesté* might cost us our heads, we ran away as quickly as we could.

This incident, apart from displaying the invincible curiosity of children and their concentration on the small points of behaviour shown by their elders, shows what little attention was paid to the safety of an important member of the Imperial family dining in the midst of a hostile Italian population. I do not know whether or not time-bombs can be made small enough; but something small and light could have been placed inside that cap to explode when it was placed on the Imperial head.

As a matter of fact, anything of the kind was foreign to the Italian population at that time. There was inevitably hostility, but this was expressed by shouting "Abasso" at appropriate occasions—"Down with the Austrians! Down with the Kaiser!" and down with everything else the Italians would have liked to see pulled down, but could not pull down.

Perhaps the greatest weakness lay in the protocol-bound behaviour of the members of the ruling house. The enforcing of archaic rules adversely affected the fate of ordinary people in the service of the Crown, who were entirely at their mercy. This, I might remark here, was particularly noticeable in the army. Regulations entitled members of the royal house to particular salutes. Ordinary saluting was not enough. A soldier who might meet one of them had to "make front", stepping quickly out of the way and standing at attention in a petrified pose until the object of this veneration had passed. I cannot imagine what would have happened had an archduke appeared in a trench during an attack; with everyone frozen in reverence, the enemy's task would have been simplified. Most probably the High Command appreciated this difficulty and kept archdukes out of the trenches during battles.

In the Austrian peacetime army, much time was spent in ceremonial drill so that all would know precisely how to behave if they encountered a member of the Imperial family. I went through this training myself. Our corporal-instructor gave great emphasis to this drill and even attempted dress rehearsals.

He would begin by saying, "I am the Archduchess Theresa Innunciata. March forward and meet me!" He would then walk towards us, moving his large feet in his clumsy boots in dainty steps like a ballerina, bending his arm as if holding a parasol and forcing his crude face into a stupid kind of grin to denote royal graciousness. He had no intention of clowning. Making fun of the Imperial family would have been a highly dangerous pastime.

It was many years later that I appreciated the nervousness shown by the junior officers at that banquet at Lavarone. As a boy I wondered why they should show so much trepidation with so much excellent food about. I was unaware that one single word of displeasure or even criticism from the Archduke would destroy a young man's career for ever. In Saxony they had a proverb: "Gehe nie zu Deinem Fuerst, wenm Du nicht gerufen wirst"— Never go to your sovereign if you are not called.

If we children had had the slightest suspicion of the tension being endured by the subalterns at the dinner party, all our sympathies would have been with them.

# CHAPTER XV

THE early years of this century marked the beginning of changes in everyday life which have not, or so I think, made life more pleasant. Although he was so powerful an influence in a new approach to his subject of study, father did not appreciate new inventions. I have already said how he disliked the telephone and never used it if this could possibly be avoided. When, a good many years later, a radio had its place in many homes, none appeared in his own part of the flat nor in the family living-room. As I shall tell later, he did listen to Schuschnigg making his abdication speech to the Austrian nation; but this is the only occasion I can recall his tolerating the radio.

He never used a typewriter himself and rarely dictated either letters or other literary work, preferring to write everything in long-hand with a large fountain-pen of the best quality which had the broadest available nib. He had no prejudice against motors when they became general nor later against aeroplanes; indeed in Berlin at the age of seventy-five he flew on a pleasure trip and enjoyed it immensely.

But I am getting somewhat ahead of my story and must return to Lavarone where the family had their first experience of motorcars. The *cavaliere* from Padova owned a Fiat and he was always delighted when he could succeed in persuading father and the family to go on small excursions. It was, of course, an open car with no protection from the weather and a maximum speed of forty kilometres an hour. I had been told that this top speed was the greatest a human being could accept without disintegration of his organs and senses, a story I had accepted without question: in consequence I kept an excited eye on the speedometer, being somewhat frustrated by the fact that it had no markings beyond forty.

Excursions in the *cavaliere*'s Fiat did allow us to pass quickly over parts of the road we already knew, and thus we could extend our walks to new and interesting places; but father was always reluctant to accept favours and for the most part we tramped along the high-road.

Sister Mathilde and father motored one day to Padova to visit the *cavaliere* in his own home. The sun was shining with great strength. Mathilde had been given a parasol of a newly invented artificial silk, an early form of nylon of which she was quite proud; but when the car stopped on a plain and she was able to get out and open the parasol to protect herself from the fierce glare, the protection did not last long. Suddenly the material disintegrated, crumbling into ashes, and Mathilde was left with a naked frame.

The Austrian army at that time was still resisting modernization. However, there were signs of a faint movement towards more up-to-date equipment. Surrounded as we were in Lavarone by troops in training for modern warfare, we were able to observe the birth-pangs of these newer ideas which were to replace the antique equipment which had already lost Austria wars, notably the war with Prussia, when her old-fashioned muzzle-loading muskets had no chance against the Prussians' then famous "needle", breech-loading gun.

Even in 1914, ordinary woollen socks were not issued to Austrian infantrymen. They were given squares of flannel and in these their feet were carefully wrapped up before being fitted into their boots. They might have been pigs' trotters served in a pork butcher's shop. These flannel squares were called *Fussfetzen* (foot rags) and the Austrian infantry soldiers of those days were referred to in a derisive sense as *Fussfetzen Indianer* (Foot-rag Indians). I might remark here that if it had not been for this contemptuous label plastered on to what is, at least in the last resort, the flower of any army, I might have joined the infantry when my term of service began: in which case my chances of survival when the First World War came would have been slender.

While we were at Lavarone we were able to observe one aspect of Austria's mild attempt to prepare for modern warfare. The army had recognized that the old method of climbing the highest tree to gain knowledge of an enemy's position was much less effective than an observation balloon, a development in other countries which then showed the beginning of deep interest in air conquest. We were the first civilians, at least in Lavarone, to watch the first attempt of the Austrian army to use an observation balloon.

A secluded spot with a supply of water was needed for the experiment, and Lavarone with its lake—water being needed to produce the gas to inflate the balloon—was ideal. Our interest was divided. Since all the windows of our rooms faced the lake, we had a grandstand view of the proceedings which were exciting enough; but the gas production poisoned the lake water and soon the small fish were all floating dead on the surface, turning their little white bellies up to the sun. Also, we had to give up swimming.

"Our" lieutenant, as we called him, the young officer who was courting Mathilde, might have been a useful source of information on the hated enterprise, if he had had much to do with the experiment or if, as he said, he knew anything about it. He added that his brother officers concerned with the work knew hardly more. They had been promised an army book of instructions but by some error the book that arrived gave careful instructions how to build a field bakery. The general opinion in the officer's mess was that this book was useless and should be sent back, but the commanding officer decided that any book was better than no book. He hoped, he said, that they might be able to use parts of it.

Two dozen infantrymen were detailed for the experiments, all Czechs, who neither spoke nor understood German beyond the regular words of command, a disability which might have been met had the regiment been able to spare the services of a bilingual N.C.O. Since none of the officers spoke the language spoken by the Czechs, the former might have been deaf and the latter dumb for all the use they could be to each other if anything went wrong and clear unexpected directions were needed.

However, as I watched from my window one day, they did succeed miraculously in inflating the balloon and even getting it to float in the air very much like the blimps the British used in London during the last war. An Austrian first lieutenant was in the gondola, while a second lieutenant remained on a meadow near the shore of the lake to direct the ground-crew.

Since the Czech ground-crew knew only command words like, "Halt!" "Present Arms!" "Fix Bayonets!" and so on, they had not the faintest idea what was being ordered when the second lieutenant shouted either "Pull down!" or "Let go!" Army regulations had been compiled long before captive balloons were invented. Thus they were driven to guess, the result being that some pulled and others slackened the lines, much to the discomfort of the first lieutenant in the gondola, which, following the erratic movements of the balloon, rolled and rocked like a small boat in a heavy sea.

I had always disliked swearing, but the blasphemies the officer in the gondola poured forth—he had a clear penetrating voice and the balloon was not very high—were quite fascinating and worth listening to.

When, somehow, the balloon was grounded and the first lieutenant emerged from the gondola, he showed his fury by grimly addressing the second lieutenant, whom he blamed for his dangerous and ridiculous ride, as "Herr Lieutenant": and no graver rebuke was possible. They had been intimate friends and I had seen them often enough when off-duty walking arm in arm and calling each other Pepi and Rudi. I might add that the night following this rock an' roll exhibition, the balloon went up in flames without hurting anyone; but we were in bed when this happened.

A statue of Sigmund Freud by the sculptor Nemon

Both these photographs show Sigmund Freud in the role of grand-father. *Above:* With Eva, Oliver's daughter. *Below:* With Stephen, Ernst's eldest son

# CHAPTER XVI

FOR me the culminating point in this holiday at Lavarone came when father, to my great delight, chose me as his companion for a walking and climbing expedition. Father had heard of a small isolated village on a mountain lake called Molveno, and the idea of visiting it to see if it would do for a family summer holiday gave an excuse for what promised to be a delightful walk. It looked promising on the map in the guidebook as a lonely and secluded spot most probably free from the fashionable crowds that father disliked so much.

Our plan was to walk from Trento to the foot of Monte Gazza, then along some picturesque valleys, to cross the mountain and to descend to the other side where we expected to find Molveno. Monte Gazza is not well known, but it is a respectable mountain reaching to about 6,000 feet.

As it turned out, the trip was most enjoyable and my few days alone with father, who usually had to be shared with so many, remain my proudest and most precious memories.

We left Lavarone at four o'clock one afternoon. Father wore a conventional country suit with a soft shirt with collar attached and a tie. My mother, who ordered all my father's clothes, tried to reach absolute perfection, always taking the greatest care in ordinary well-cut clothes made from British cloth. Thus he appeared as respectable as he did in Vienna in his dark suits and black ties. Both of us had rucksacks and both wore suitably nailed boots. Father carried a strong walking-stick with an iron spike while I had the long straight *Alpenstock*, a most useful tool which is now completely out of fashion and would, I imagine, make a modern mountaineer look a little ridiculous.

As a contrast to my parent's respectable appearance, I wore well-used leather shorts and the usual Tyrolean outfit. Although I was only sixteen, I was taller than my father and very thin at that time. I must have looked a strange sight and I am certain that without my distinguished-looking companion, I would not have been admitted to the good hotels he chose in which to spend our nights.

We marched the twelve odd miles down from Lavarone on that boiling hot August day on the broad excellent road built by the Austrians for strategic reasons—easy going, all downhill with little traffic to disturb us, although we overtook a number of mule-drawn vehicles and occasionally encountered troops, infantry on route marches looking sun-burnt, dusty and tired. We pitied them, and they probably pitied us.

Because father had a horror of missing a train or a boat, it was seldom that he reached a station or any other point of departure less than half an hour early; and so we reached Caldonazzo with plenty of time to enjoy sweet black coffee in a charming road-side inn.

The train journey from Caldonazzo to Trento was not pleasant because although father had booked places in the second class, the train was packed with officers from various mountain garrisons on their way to Trento, and we had to stand in the corridor. It was dark when we reached our destination and the good hotel where father had booked a room, but we had no sooner got rid of our rucksacks than we were again out exploring the town, enjoying a first look at the famous Dome and the Dante Monument. After a short view of the town, father found a first-class restaurant where we enjoyed an excellent dinner.

Looking back, I am filled with respect for the energy of my father, who was in his fiftieth year. We had started the day early with the usual three to four hours' walk through the Lavarone forests, and much of the afternoon had been spent tramping through the ankle-deep dust of the strategic road leading to Caldonazzo. We must have covered at least thirty miles. I was perhaps too excited to feel any fatigue, but as for father, he obviously never got tired.

After dinner we returned to the Dome, where he explained the architecture and stylistic development which could be read on the magnificent building. He was a wonderful teacher; I doubt if a better one existed in our century; and although after so long a day this was hardly the time for a lecture on architecture and history, his class of one remained absorbed and in awe.

However, as I listened, my mind must have eventually wandered a little because I remember being interested in the shadows which a street lamp behind us cast on the walls of the cathedral. There was father's shadow—a broad-shouldered, well-proportioned shadow; there was my silhouette, very long and very thin, but, and I was delighted, the shapes of our heads appeared to be very much alike: a youthful appraisal, of course; but even then, at sixteen, I was merely contemplating outer shapes. It could not occur to me to compare their contents.

The hotel manager had given us a magnificent room on the ground floor facing the street, a compliment to father, I think; but like some kindly intention it went wrong in effect. I do not know what Trento citizens do during the day; they appear to be suitably quiet and orderly in their dim shops and offices, seldom venturing on to the streets which are as hot as ovens; but when darkness falls, they appear to wake up with great ebullience and, apparently, to regard the area of the hotel as the best promenade.

Silent nights were not for the citizens of Trento; they called to each other at the top of their voices; they sang loudly and unmelodiously in their guttural Trentino dialect and the result was, according to my diary, father slept for one restless hour, while I did not sleep at all. My diary makes up for this severe criticism of the nocturnal habits of the people by asking in its carefully written schoolboy hand, "What is one sleepless night against the pleasure and honour of being out on an excursion with father, and having him all to myself?"

The sleepless night did not in any way affect us and we were up before sunrise ready to start without breakfast but with my rucksack rather heavily packed with provisions ordered from the hotel.

That was a wonderful morning. The stimulus of the cool morning air gave spring to our feet and we felt ourselves to be more than ever happy and willing slaves to wanderlust as we marched briskly along the highway, passing villas and palaces with their marble statues relieved by slim cypresses; and sometimes we passed humbler dwellings, farm-houses, yet picturesque with their attendant chestnut- and mulberry-trees and surrounding vineyards. Wanderlust, I think, so far as it rules over earth, recruits many more inner continental people than seafaring races.

We passed through the narrow gorge of the Vela, a mountain torrent, where in its narrowest point a strong fortification has been built into the rock. Emerging from the gorge, we were out again in the sunshine of the wide open valley with its splendour of sub-tropical vegetation. Both of us being in high spirits, this was clearly the moment for a marching song but not, alas, for the Freuds. I do not think my father could isolate one melody from another and I had inherited this deficiency, a great disadvantage in a musical country like Austria. I might remark here that as far as I was concerned this tone-deafness, I suppose one might call it, could have landed me in more trouble than it did when I served in an Austrian mounted troop if it had not been for my horse. Signals were given by bugle, which conveyed no order to my brain; I had to depend on my horse to obey them with military precision: which he did very nicely.

We had coffee in a roadside house near a village called Cadine and from here we could see Monte Gazza as we began eating the food supplied by the Trento hotel. After a short rest, we were on the march again, passing the lonely lake of Terlago and leaving the road leading south to Castell Toblino, a place, incidentally, father had visited some years earlier and which he had described as of dreamlike beauty. This road which we had left follows the valley of the Sarca and the Gardasee. We now took narrow lanes which finally led to a stony footpath mounting the lower slopes of Mount Gazza.

My father on his frequent excursions with us children had laid down certain simple rules when climbing steep mountain pathways. One should keep a fair distance between oneself and the person ahead; one should not talk; one should not often stop to rest and never to sit down to rest; and, above all, one should be very careful not to loosen stones which might disturb, or even endanger, those following behind.

Our surroundings had now lost their soft beauty. There was nothing but stone and parched bush and thorn, no shade and, of course, no water anywhere. The sun had risen high in the sky and we were fully exposed to its pitiless glare. Nature appeared to be dead from exhaustion. Even the lizards had abandoned running up and down boulders and were, doubtless, resting in holes or crevices.

Following our rule of keeping a fair distance between us as we climbed the steep stony pathway, I was some twenty paces ahead of father, or I imagined I was when I looked back to see how he was getting along. He had vanished. The only sound that had disturbed the silence of the mountain, the clatter of his stick on the stones, had ceased.

I had never in my life been asked to face an emergency and it did not occur to me to consider one now as I turned to run down the steep pathway. Father might have stepped aside to gain a better view. I could think of many reasons but not the one that now confronted me.

He was leaning against a boulder near a low bush. His face was a purple red, almost violet, and he seemed incapable of talking. He was able to point towards my rucksack, and I guessed that he was indicating the bottle of Chianti I carried. Pulling out the flask and kneeling beside him, I handed him the flask. With his arms raised and bending backwards, he drank deeply from the actual bottle. Anxiously I studied his face which, although still discoloured, remained as calm as it always was. He had not for a moment lost his self-control.

Nevertheless, and this was notable in my father, he did for once abandon a number of conventions which he always strictly observed. He drank from the actual bottle instead of using the small flat aluminium beaker he carried in his waistcoat pocket. He removed his tie and unbuttoned his collar. He did not, however, go so far as to take off his coat.

It was a difficult situation for a boy of sixteen who had led so sheltered a life, and I had no idea what to do. I might have run to the nearest village, but since my Italian was limited to "buona sera" and "caffè nero" it would have been difficult to make myself understood.

Fortunately, before I could decide what to do, father recovered from this heat-stroke, and after a little while he looked and talked as if nothing had happened.

We now held a council-of-war to decide what to do. I was flattered when my opinion was asked and I gave my views emphatically: Monte Gazza should be left alone; it was neither an interesting nor a beautiful mountain; there must be other ways of reaching Molveno.

I was supposed to have carefully studied the map before we started on this tour but, if the truth must be told, I had been too lazy to do so. Thus much mental agility was needed to hide this fact and to answer intelligently when father began explaining the rather involved route we should now have to follow if we would reach Molveno that day. I do not think I was found out, but even as I followed the explanations and gave my assent, I felt very guilty and resolved to make up for this at the first possible moment, to study the map thoroughly. I kept this resolve, half a century later: a few days ago in fact.

We retraced our steps back down the steep stony pathway and across the bleak desert, passing through small mountain hamlets until we were back at the village of Terlago. Here was a pleasant inn where we decided to have a meal and a rest. At this point, or so it seems as I look back on our journey, the adventure really ended. From now on we did not earn that contentment and peace tramping gives; we became no longer self-dependent, and the fatigue of the road or mountain pathway was not there to reward us with rest at the end of the day. I cannot say that these were my thoughts when father decided to order a carriage. The prospect of driving about in one drawn by horses with father beside me promised to be exciting and full of interest.

While the innkeeper's wife led us out to the house-garden where she began to spread a snowy table-cloth over the rough board table under a chestnut-tree, treating us with that appealing Italian *gentilezza*, the innkeeper busied himself in the stables, grooming the horses and dusting the carriage.

I have not inherited my father's delight in archaeology and his deep interest in Greek and Roman antiquities; but having been educated, as he was, in a humanistic gymnasium, a grammar school I expect one might call it in English, where Latin and Greek were given great emphasis, I had accepted, as had he, the beauty of Homer's epics, and the heroes of the *Iliad* and the *Odyssey* lived in my imagination when I was a boy. Thus in this remote and isolated mountain village, we could easily imagine ourselves back in the world of Odysseus and Priam. There were no tins of sardines nor soda-water syphons to remind us that we were in the twentieth century.

The innkeeper's wife wore a chain of copper coins around her neck and she had sandals on her bare feet. Through the open door of the large kitchen we could see a big copper kettle hanging over a fire, and slices of meat were roasting gently on sticks. On the table was a basket of figs and olives. When all was ready we, like the ancient heroes, "lifted our hands to the well-prepared feast".

When the carriage was ready we guessed that the innkeeper had chosen his best pair of horses, and it was plain that he had worked hard on them with his brushes and curry-comb. Their coats shone as bravely as those of the *Lippizaners* of the Imperial stables of Vienna.

We had to return to Trento by the same road we had enjoyed so much that morning, our strong fresh horses covering the distance, now downhill, at what seemed incredible speed.

Driving northwards through the dusty valley of the Adige we reached Mezzolombardo, where we took another carriage and began following a steep road which passed through the villages of Fai and Andalo and descended to our destination, the Lake of Molveno.

This luxurious mode of travel must have cost father a small fortune, probably as much as he got from his publishers for one of his more important books. However, he never expressed the slightest objection, nor did he even raise the subject of money when talking to me. That was not his way.

After driving in carriages for more than eight hours, we found ourselves very late in reaching Molveno. The result was that by chance the only hotel in the place was already full and all we could be given was what my diary calls "a room without windows"—an attic most probaby. This was exchanged the next day for a pleasant double room.

The hotel was about half a mile distant from the picturesque but rather poor and dilapidated village of Molveno. The last part of the road was only a rough track. Today, fifty years later, the lake is encircled by modern motor roads and there is a variety of accommodation—one first-class hotel, two second-class, three third-class and three fourth-class. There is also now a chair-lift to one of the lesser neighbouring mountains of about 5,000 feet.

The lake is dominated by the steep rocky walls of the Brenta group which rise upwards of 10,000 feet and offer some of the grandest, as well as the most dangerous, rock-climbing in the Dolomites. As will be suspected without difficulty, I am here quoting freely from an Italian brochure written with much more abandon and charm than my sternly written schoolboy diary can offer.

The fact that when we were at Molveno the place remained, comparatively speaking, immune to the rush of tourists which, in the opinion of some quiet people seems to disguise the lovely face of nature, should have made Molveno attractive to father; but although we had quite a good time there, he did not seem to like the place very much. I have a feeling that Molveno was affected at least somewhat by the unpleasant event of that morning which forced us to use the legs of horses instead of our own. Perhaps a better reason lay in the hotel kitchen. We had sensed, when first being greeted by the manager, that something was rotten in the state of Molveno. Possibly the cook had run away and could not be quickly replaced except by, perhaps, the boiler-man. The food served to us looked peculiar and had a peculiar smell, being hardly eatable.

We had the place, the lake and its surroundings, much to ourselves, because the guests who had crowded out the hotel the night before were all mountaineers, who, by the time we were having breakfast on the hotel balcony, were doubtless fighting for their lives in rope-soled shoes with forty yards of manila rope slung around their chest and shoulders on the vertical walls of the Guglia di Brenta.

We tramped the few miles around the lake, father looking in vain for the kind of forest he loved, but only finding odd patches of fir-trees high on isolated rocky and mossy ground. We took one of the rowing-boats and tried a little fishing, but without any particular success that I can recall although father, who handled his fishing-rod with his usual skill—much greater than his sons'— did his best. Fishing, however, was never one of father's greatest passions, like collecting mushrooms or alpine flowers. Although the water of the lake was really melted ice, since it had come from the mountains above and was crystal clear, it was quite warm and we enjoyed the swim we had very much.

Father was a fair, if somewhat orthodox, swimmer, never changing from a formal breast-stroke, always rather handicapped by trying to keep his beard out of the water. I wore a beard myself in my early fifties, and I know how difficult it is to get a thoroughly wet beard neat and tidy after one has been diving and swimming under water a lot: not, I fear, that failure gave me a moment's worry.

The sun leaves Molveno fairly early and vanishes behind the steep mountain walls, turning the rocks into rather grim silhouettes which doubtless have beauty of their own but are, in effect, forbidding and depressing, certainly when compared with the wide horizon and beautiful sunsets of Lavarone. I was affected in this way, but it might be only fair to Molveno to suggest that the poor food at the hotel was more to blame. I know that after walking, taking the train, and making our way up the strategic road back to Lavarone, I was put to bed with a severe bout of indigestion and remained there for a day or two. Father was as fit and well as ever.

# CHAPTER XVII

OWING to the altitude of Lavarone, autumn comes early with unpleasantly cold nights, and so, towards the end of August, our parents decided to follow the sun, actually to the Lake of Garda where summer still remained in full swing.

We left early in the morning on the last day of August 1906. Today, such a journey would mean little to children: they would be packed into a car and off they would go at great speed with little hope of adventure. An hour or so's rush in a car would see the exchange of one place for another and the journey would have only the slightest place in their memories.

It was very different in 1906 and infinitely more exciting. We were carried in two horse-drawn vehicles, landaus in fact. Although I have travelled much since in a variety of ways, by rail, by car, by plane, in steamers and, on the whole, enjoyed them all, that journey from Lavarone to Lake Garda remains the most delightful journey of my life. Today one can still recapture the same charm in small canoes and on horseback.

Father and mother sat side by side in the comfortable back seat of one landau with little Anna between them, and Mathilde on the seat facing them. This carriage, being lightly loaded, was drawn by a pair of horses. The second carriage, piled high with the enormous amount of baggage that always accompanied the family, carried the rest of the children and was drawn by four horses. To my own great satisfaction, I was given a seat on the box next to the driver.

Both drivers were Italian, merry, gentle and full of fun. The road was several inches thick with dust and, to protect them from flies, the horses wore nets over their harness and their heads were decorated with many multi-coloured tassels and an array of little bells. The tassels disturbed the flies, but the object of the bells was to warn approaching vehicles on the narrow winding road, but evidently not quite enough for the drivers, for when approaching corners they added to the cheerful din by shouting at their horses and cracking their whips.

It is quite a long journey from Lavarone to Lake Garda, about twenty-five miles, and so the coachmen drove their horses at their best speed to permit them to return to Lavarone that same day and thus to save the expense of stabling at an inn. It was much too early in the century to permit me to compare our dashing progress with a film scene of stage-coaches being pursued by bandits or Red Indians, but when I have seen such, I easily recall our glorious rush down the roads that day between Lavarone and Lake Garda.

The going was, on the whole, easy on the horses because it was always downhill; and, of course, it got warmer and warmer as the day progressed. Soon our faces were white with dust, which seemed to concentrate on our eyelashes until we hardly knew each other.

It demands great skill to drive four horses at a canter on a narrow winding road, and our driver was an artist at his job; also he was very good-tempered, a great advantage especially when affection for his beasts is combined with firmness. His whip was never used to punish: it was a brilliant cracking device. However, he was not sparing in admonitions when slackened traces showed that a horse was not doing his fair share. Such a horse was fiercely admonished by name in a fiery shout possibly intermixed with curses, something I could not be sure of since my knowledge of Italian was not good enough to translate this one-sided conversation. The guilty horse's knowledge of Italian must have been excellent because he invariably accepted the rebuke and promptly did better.

Our carriage led the procession fairly well ahead of father's and mother's to save them from some of the dust we raised. This forced our driver to look back occasionally to avoid losing contact. From time to time we paused to give the horses a rest and on one of these occasions the driver of the second landau jumped over a low wall surrounding a vineyard and helped himself to some bunches of ripe dark-blue grapes. Sister Mathilde tells me that when he offered these to father, father asked him how much he owed for the grapes, so welcome on that warm journey. Father was told that nothing had to be paid: the offering was made on behalf of *gentilezza*.

The fact that the grapes had obviously been stolen did not in any way affect the *gentilezza* of the gesture, and I confess that my conscience was in no way affected when I enjoyed my share of the gift.

It was all exciting and enjoyable, but I cannot now remember the precise route we followed nor the names of the villages we passed through, my diary confining itself to an account of Rovereto and its best hotel where we paused for a rest and a mid-day meal. The hotel boasted a magnificent hall of Moorish architecture with allegorical frescoes and a fountain in what I recorded as "Arabic-Byzantine style". I was most impressed, and I confided to my diary that when I had a villa of my own, I would have a similar fountain in its garden. Hitler's arrival in Austria prevented this dream from coming true and, in any case, I am not sure that fountains in suburban gardens are fashionable today.

September on the Gardasee is the best time of the year, I think, to enjoy the superb beauty of the region. The extreme heat of the summer has been exchanged for a balmy atmosphere which makes walking a particular delight and, best of all, the local fruit is ripe—grapes, peaches, figs and olives. The weather remained perfect during the several weeks we stayed there: there was hardly ever a cloud in the dark-blue sky.

Our hotel, situated on the road between Riva and Torbole, was rather old-fashioned and its rooms not particularly comfortable, but its garden of not less than five acres which swept down to the lake was magnificent with an abundance of fruit-trees and vines, the latter forming fruitful pergolas. It was only ten minutes' walk to the centre of Riva, and nearly every morning father took us to the market-place where the fruit was plentiful and cheap.

A row of plane-trees bordered the lake, and hotel guests had the private use of a small jetty jutting out into the transparently blue water for bathing.

Father had several guests to stay with him at this time, amongst them being Uncle Alexander and Professor Koenigstein, the latter being that cheerful, forceful and most attractive friend who had won the hearts of us children at Koenigsee when he climbed my private rock with so much ease and grace. At Riva we could again admire his swimming. With his broad shoulders and greying beard he could easily have posed for a statue of Neptune. He was not only a good sportsman: he was a good sport in every sense of the word.

Professor Koenigstein had a deep voice and a masterful, but not unattractive, way of handling people: thus in the Viennese circles of Jewish intellectuals he was highly respected and invariably chosen as president of the different associations. No one else had his superb ability to preside at meetings and to manage their progress with the least amount of digression. My mother occasionally repeated what was often said in Vienna: "Societies may come and go, but Professor Koenigstein always remains in the president's chair."

Father took us for an excursion one day to the southern end of the lake, to Sirmione, where we visited the grotto of Catullus and some Roman relics. Uncle Alexander was with us. It was a stormy day and the small paddle-steamer made heavy weather of the steep seas which quickly rise in any wind on a big lake. She pitched and rolled considerably and a party of Italian women in the second class became very seasick, some of them even panicking and kneeling in prayer to be saved from the watery grave they feared was opening around them. We Freud children were good sailors, and I am afraid the agony of mind suffered by the poor Italian women, instead of awakening sympathy, only amused us.

Father took us all down to lunch in the saloon of the ship. We could not expect a good meal in the stuffy cabin of a rolling and pitching paddle-steamer with a small galley; but the indifference of the fare extended to the dessert course when, in a district where grows the best fruit in Europe, we were served with a bowl of half-green windfall apples that were slightly decayed.

Characteristically, Uncle Alexander, who could not tolerate the suspicion of being swindled, promptly sent for the waiter, who only came reluctantly after uncle had raised his voice above the clatter of the engines and the howling of the storm.

"You call this fruit?" shouted Uncle Alexander. "You call this dessert? This is fit for swine—*pro porci*!"

"Not *pro porci*," said father calmly—"*pro pesci*", and with an elegant movement he threw the bowl of rotten apples through the porthole to the fish.

I do not think there were many children of middle-class parents at that time who enjoyed the freedom we enjoyed or accepted quite naturally the trust shown in us by our parents. Nevertheless, although we missed father very much when he left us towards the end of the holiday at Riva, we had a wonderful time, misusing our freedom and independence but seldom.

I am sure everybody will admit that the spirit of adventure is very strong in healthy, normal growing boys and that nothing makes them happier than to be free from guidance—parental or otherwise—no matter how gently and tactfully such guidance is shown.

One thinks of the awful fate endured by princes and heirs to thrones who are never allowed, so far as I know, to be free to enjoy what we enjoyed—going out alone or in pairs to have adventures often of our own imagining but yet having the texture of reality. My companion was my brother Ernst, two years younger than me: in 1906 he was fourteen years old.

The wishful dreamings of boys today appear to be deeply con-cerned with space-ships which can take them to other worlds. The minds of boys of 1906 reached only to travelling across the sea to foreign lands. Lake Garda, being large enough to disappear over the horizon when seen from Riva, supplied us with an ocean apparently as wide as the world and, of course, a foreign country, Italy, was only a few miles distant.

We had learnt from experience on other lakes that rowing can be entertaining for a limited time but that progress after the first few energetic spurts can be very slow. When we discovered a mast seven or eight feet long and a rolled-up sail tucked under the seat of the small rowing-boat we were allowed to use at Riva, our exploring prospects brightened. Of sails and sailing we knew nothing; but an Irishman staying at the hotel with his daughter came to our aid when he saw us vainly attempting to step the mast and to fix the sail. He showed us how to plunge the mast through a hole in the seat to rest in its seating in the keel, how to tighten the mast stays and, finally, how to set the simple sail and how to control its boom with the main-sheet which, he insisted, should never be tied: some hand had to hold it if disaster were to be avoided on the high seas. I might remark here that the Irish accent was somewhat strange to us and differed widely from the

Austrian-English we had been taught; but we were able to follow him very well.

We found with surprise and pleasure that our little boat went with the wind in the sail, carrying us along speedily and obeying the rudder provided we were sailing with the wind. Any attempts at variation in direction were not successful, because we never mastered the art of sailing up into the wind by an artful use of the main-sheet and rudder.

Fortunately, nature on Lake Garda favours boys without seafaring traditions. During normal good weather the directions of winds remain constant. Every morning a breeze from the northward called *tramontana*—over the mountains—blew down the lake for several hours, dying down just before noon. At about three o'clock in the afternoon a much stronger breeze came from the south. This was called the *ora*.

Thus it never really became necessary for us to attempt any tacking, or even to beat up into the wind. Riva, of course, was still in Austria; but some miles to the southward was Italy and since there was then no need for passports or identity papers, and because the local winds were so conveniently arranged, the *tramontana* carried us easily to Italy before lunch and the *ora* brought us back to Austria in the afternoon.

We were still very young and inexperienced in sailing, but mother offered no objection to our sailing to Limone, about eight miles from Riva, and even to Malcesine, about fourteen miles away. When we explained that, being dependent on the winds, we could not return for lunch, she had sandwiches and fruit packed for us. Although sailing on Lake Garda seemed the laziest sport we had hitherto enjoyed, it made us very hungry and the sandwiches and fruit were welcome. And thus we sailed, taking turns, one of us with his hand on the tiller, the other holding the main-sheet and watching that the sail got its full share of wind. Because we were not too happy in the art of manœuvring a sailing-ship entering port, we found it safest to let down the sail and to row the last few hundred yards.

Limone was a very small and poor village whose only claim to fame was that it is the most northerly point in Europe where lemons will grow out of doors, actually on terraces. A boy of about our own age helped us to moor our boat and then presented us with a branch of a lemon-tree on which the lemons, some ripe, some still green, remained. We were glad to have something to take back to mother as a present, and the boy accepted our small tip with Italian grace.

The boy, Salvatore was his name, decided to be our guide; but since we knew little Italian, what he had to say about the few objects of interest meant nothing to us and he became something of a nuisance we could not shake off. Suddenly, in the middle of his Italian explanations, he broke off and said in what seemed to us fluent German, "We are now very good friends, and we must write to each other postcards and letters frequently. When I come to Vienna [we had told him we came from that city], I must visit you and stay at your house."

Until we realized that these phrases were repeated parrot-fashion, that their meaning meant nothing whatever to the Italian boy, we thought this might be taking advantage of a very short acquaintance.

At a moment when we were wondering how we could get rid of him without appearing to be rude, the leaves of the surrounding lemon-trees began stirring, at first very softly but soon with insistence. The *ora* had come to blow us home again and we hurried to our boat.

As we were making ready, another small boat carrying German-speaking people arrived to see the lemons. Salvatore was ready for them with his branch of lemons and to say, as we heard him, "We are very good friends and we must write postcards to each other...."

The trip to Malcesine, a much bigger place with several hotels and a useful harbour, was more eventful. Brother Ernst, drunk with pride and bravado, an intoxication induced by his belief in our seamanship, allowèd himself to wave and to shout a greeting to Italian customs officials in a motor patrol-boat at a moment when we were close to the frontier.

Since there remain in our family traditions two versions of what Ernst shouted, and because I do not want to start a quarrel between two elderly and dignified gentlemen, brothers always on brotherly and affectionate terms, I offer both versions. Ernst insists that he merely shouted something like "How do you do?" in both German and Italian. My version is that he shouted, "We

My father in his study surrounded by Greek and Egyptian antiquities,
with the chow Jofi, his constant companion

Marie Bonaparte taking a snapshot of Sigmund Freud in his study are the boldest and most clever smugglers on the whole lake, but you will never catch us."

There is evidence that my version is perhaps not far wrong in the fact that we were promptly overhauled by the patrol-boat, ordered to stop and thoroughly searched. All they found was two empty Chianti bottles not ours, and the remains of our lunch, probably the cheese sandwiches which we had left to the last, preferring the other varieties. We were soon sent on our way again.

Quite cocksure in our seamanship, one day we invited our little sister Anna to join us, possibly to impress her with our efficiency as sailors. She came trustfully and, I may say, she recalls the incident better than I do.

The south wind had freshened and a sea was rising, but this meant nothing to sailors like Ernst and me, not until we found our little ship becoming quite disobedient and doing what she liked without reference to whatever we attempted to do with the tiller and main-sheet. Soon we were being driven much too close to the rocks of the western shore.

My sister Anna recalls that her brothers asked her to lie flat in the bottom of the boat, evidently, I suppose, to save her head from being struck by the boom which was flying from side to side. It sounds rather a polite request at this distance until it is recalled that big brothers under these circumstances do not usually "ask" little sisters to do something: Anna was most probably sternly ordered to lie down. She recalls that she accepted the command gladly since she was enjoying the adventure tremendously and was not a bit afraid. We Freud children had inherited a precious gift from both our parents: we enjoyed freedom from fear. Anna had received a big portion, something proved many years later when the Nazis invaded Austria.

Fortunately, we were seen by mother as we pitched and rolled in the growing sea, our sail flapping backwards and forwards in a most reckless way. She promptly hailed the nearest sailing-boat moored at the boating-pier and waiting to be hired. Stepping on board, she ordered it to the rescue. By this time we had taken down the sail. In truth, it was really good sailing weather for sailors, something Ernst and I realized with a consequent fall of our pride when mother's rescue vessel came skimming over the waves effortlessly. Mother's ship, with elegance and ease, escorted us to the safety of the small rocky port of Ponale, while we, in our water-laden boat, were forced to row against the wind and current with all our strength.

Many mothers, I expect, would have been seriously upset over such an incident, especially when left in sole charge of a family. She, alone of the family, was a poor sailor: thus her coming to our rescue showed superb courage. Also, we had been very silly in putting to sea when white horses were already riding over the lake in dense squadrons. Inexperience was our only excuse, something we had to admit to ourselves without prompting. As was usual in such cases in my family, there were no recriminations, no dramatizing, and the event was quickly forgotten.

To finish the story of the holiday at Riva I must recall one other incident. One day I set out alone to explore the desolate and mountainous country surrounding a lonely lake. This meant following a road which was often cut deeply through rock, thus forming what amounted to long gloomy tunnels. These tunnels were depressing enough during the afternoon, but bathed in threatening darkness on my return, they seemed to form a perfect setting for a murder or at least a robbery with violence. As I was negotiating one of the last tunnels, I saw coming towards me in the dim light the shape of a man. He had detected me at the same moment because I saw him stop and press himself against the wall. A robber, I decided. Although I had nothing he could rob me of, I determined to defend myself to the death. I took out my pocket-knife and snapped it open to its fixed position with a loud click. Then, slinging a handkerchief around my wrist, I marched resolutely forward, a menacing figure in that light because, although only sixteen, I was very tall for my age.

As I advanced, the shadow of the unknown robber moved forward as well. I saw that he was cringing closely to the opposite wall in a most alarming manner. But when he reached a point level with me, he took to his heels and ran like a madman, vanishing in the darkness. I felt ashamed of this adventure when I reached home, suspecting that mother and my sisters and brothers would have difficulty in deciding which of the imaginary robbers had been more frightened, and so I decided not to tell them. However, I did confide in a most attractive American girl who was staying at the hotel, a girl with whom I had become quite friendly to the extent of what might have been called flirtation had we been a year or two older. She—her name was Julia—was as romantic as I was: and so she heard my story with deep interest and womanly sympathy, absolving me of all guilt and giving a verdict which I thought heartening. She said I had acted with prudence and courage, that under such circumstances an American boy would have behaved in precisely the same way.

Like many of her countrymen at this time, Julia and her parents had travelled a great deal on the Continent, and a story she told me made a deep and lasting impression on my mind. They were Jews and, unaccustomed to any kind of discrimination against their race, they crossed the Russian frontier. They were stopped by the Russian customs officials and sent back in a most humiliating manner. Jews at that time were not allowed to travel freely in Russia.

The story infuriated me, and I hoped that one day I would cross the Russian frontier without that special permission needed for people of my race. My hopes were realized when, as an Austrian ensign during the First World War, I crossed in triumph. Much has happened since those days; the frontier is again closed, but not against Jews only.

# CHAPTER XVIII

NINETEEN HUNDRED AND NINE was the last full summer holiday I spent with my parents and brothers and sisters. I had, to everybody's surprise, passed my matriculation examination with full honours, something of a miracle, it seemed, performed by a backward and usually unsuccessful pupil. I had now, in a sense, become of age with the right to go where I pleased for my holidays, a privilege I was not opposed to. Father was most generous with the money he gave me for holidays, so generous in fact that I often felt he gave me too much, and I felt ashamed. I frequently joined the family during holidays as a guest for a short or long period and this went on until 1914, when the First World War marked the end of our happy, carefree, and even luxurious way of life.

But to return to 1909, our last holiday together as a complete family. We went to Ammerwald, to an hotel on the Austrian-Bavarian frontier in densely wooded mountain country. The place was more a hunting centre of the Bavarian royal house than a tourist resort. It is in this area that the famous King Ludwig of Bavaria built his fairy-tale castles at immense expense until his internment as a demented person put an end to his dream-castle building activities. I believe that opinion remains divided as to whether this was an act of justice and necessity or the climax of a cruel intrigue.

King Ludwig had been an admirer and an intimate friend of Wagner, and it was in the great composer's honour that he built the Hunding-Huette which stood only a short easy walk from our hotel and in Bavaria. This wooden, thatched hut was supposed to represent the kind of dwelling inhabited by Wagner's heroes. In fact it was not very interesting and I suspect that much of its popularity could be traced to its close neighbour, a delightful forest tavern where excellent Bavarian beers were served.

We were the only people from Vienna staying at the Hotel Ammerwald, most of the other guests being South Germans from

Bavaria and the Rhineland. They appeared to be of an easy-going and not unpleasant type.

We became friendly with a South German family, about the same size as our own, headed by a father who was the manager of an important industrial concern in Düsseldorf. Father got along well with this gentleman, who was evidently a well-educated and intelligent man, and the two were often seen walking together in the pleasant grounds of the hotel in animated conversation. The rest of the guests seemed to concentrate their attention on the young *Postfraeulein,* the young woman in charge of the small post office attached to the hotel. She was attractive, efficient and resolute. All her movements were noted and discussed by the guests. With whom had she been out the previous evening for a long walk in the forest? At what time had she got back? Had she looked happier when she returned, or only just the same? Father and mother were not interested in this gossip. As an entertainment, gossip was confined to cooks and chambermaids in our home.

The affairs of the *Postfraeulein* were pushed into the background when the eldest son of the South German manager had an accident sufficiently serious, or so it seemed at first, to unite all the guests at the Ammerwald Hotel into one large sympathetic family.

This young man was a student, like myself, but with an important difference. One of the most feudally inspired corps of South Germany had accepted him as a member, and this corps was on intimate and friendly terms with the Bonner Borussia, to which belonged members of the House of Hohenzollern. Membership of such a corps was at this time an enormous advantage to a young man since it could ensure him a brilliant career. From these exclusive corps came Germany's leaders.

In consequence, this young man's membership in his corps was the centre and controlling interest of his life. His loyalty to its traditions of conduct and the esteem this would win had more importance than the passing of his examinations at the university. A student expelled through disgracing himself in a duel, or behaving badly during a drinking bout, or indeed for any other reason, lost all chance of progress in life. The young man's family were extremely proud of their son and brother and never missed a chance of mentioning his membership in the famous corps.

One day this student, accompanied by a young cousin, decided to climb a nearby mountain with the unattractive name of the Vulture's Head. It rose steeply above the narrow valley in which the hotel stood. The climb was not a formidable one if simple precautions were taken; indeed the student was perhaps justified in regarding the Vulture's Head as rather a third-class kind of mountain, and, as I see it today if not then, it was natural enough for a member of his exclusive corps to look on this expedition with youthful nonchalance and a lack of respect which, had he known it, even third-class mountains do not really like. He did not wear nailed boots: rubber-soled tennis shoes to his mind would be good enough for the Vulture's Head.

The result, or perhaps it was only an unhappy chance, was that in attempting a short-cut down the mountain on the return journey, the student slipped on a long steep slope of rubble, ending this involuntary descent sprawled out in a valley and fairly seriously hurt, certainly enough to make it impossible to move without great pain. He was able to shout to his young boy companion, urging him to get back to the hotel to raise an alarm. The boy, much more cautious, managed to slide down the slope and eventually reached the hotel.

Now while the hotel guests could boast amongst their members excellent singers, zither players and experts at skittles, there was not an experienced mountaineer amongst them. A call for volunteers to form a rescue party consequently failed. I volunteered and, I think, if left to myself I might easily have been of some use. But the hotel guests, appreciating that after all I was hardly more than a boy, objected to my going alone. I was much too shy and polite to protest when it was decided to send with me one of our own family guests, a young fellow not much older than myself but big, wise and strong and much more experienced socially. He knew nothing about rock-climbing and I feared he would be clumsy and useless. There was no question in my mind regarding his ability to handle the most difficult situation when once we reached the student; but between us and the hurt student there were only two ways of convenient and quick approach: up the very steep slope of rubble, easy enough to slide down on, but offering a difficult ascent; or by a rocky ravine which needed some skill to overcome.

All the guests, with the best will in the world, now busied themselves in preparing us for our departure, the result being that our rucksacks were soon overladen with rugs and a wide variety of foods of all kinds. I was glad when my friend rejected a very neat table-lamp fed by a battery and a number of books which would serve to entertain the student during the night which, it was felt, he would have to spend on the mountain; and even the well-meaning guests saw that an alarm clock set at an early hour for the following morning, offered by one kind lady, could be done without. As we were starting, the student's father thrust into my hands a number of packets of a particular brand of cigarette, explaining that his son was a chain-smoker who would now be out of supplies of his favourite brand and must be in an agony.

Off we started, and it was now getting late in the afternoon; but, alas, we did not get very far. We tried both ways, immediately failing on the slope of rubble and then struggling with the rocky ravine. Alone, I might have managed the former; certainly I could have climbed the latter; but my companion, very much heavier than myself, had to be dragged up difficult sections of the way. Our heavy loads of comforts which we had dared not refuse added to our difficulties. The situation that now developed was in one way amusing: when my companion and I were out together people thought he was sent to look after me because he looked so much older, a full-grown man in fact, although, as I said before, the difference in our ages was not great. After a long struggle, it became clear to both of us that together we could not possibly reach the injured lad before darkness added to our difficulties. We had made very little real progress.

I could have gone on alone, but I was dissuaded by my companion who, knowing me well, was aware that if I found the student badly hurt and needing first-aid I would be helpless. Secretly I felt that to find him seriously injured would be less frightening than to find him merely immobilized by a slight injury like a sprained ankle. I did not relish the thought of spending the night alone with one who was haughty and arrogant and who throughout a long night would treat me with the polite condescension he so often inflicted.

And so we decided to return, both being thoroughly exhausted, without thinking to sample some of the foods and drinks in our heavily laden rucksacks. I was considerably surprised to discover how very disappointed father was in my failure. He did not blame me, merely remarking that had we reached the student, the family would have celebrated the occasion with a bottle of champagne. This was a great deal from father. The only occasion I can recall the Freuds celebrating with champagne was the silver wedding of the parents. Clearly he had taken my failure very much to heart.

At first I could not understand why. I think the truth is that he wanted to be proud of me, to see me, even before the small and not distinguished company of guests at the hotel, the hero of the day. Reflecting on this later and knowing how utterly indifferent he was to all honours conferred on himself, a man lacking in vanity if ever there was one, I saw that he was ambitious for his children. I regretted that, with the best will in the world, I had on this occasion let him down. At the time, I merely regretted that my companion and I, so thoroughly exhausted on our way back, had not eaten some of the cold chicken in aspic we had carried so far.

The hotel manager had taken steps to arrange for an efficient rescue team to start off the next day, but in the meantime he had sent the hotel "boots" on an independent rescue attempt. The "boots" knew the Vulture's Head well. He had the good sense to climb the mountain by the usual tourists' footpath and to descend by the way taken by the unfortunate student. He found him without difficulty, lying in a shallow sandy ravine, and made him as comfortable as possible, spending the night with him: which was no hardship since the night was dry, calm and warm. The young man's arm had been broken and this caused great pain; but all he wanted was a drink of water. The "boots" found a trickle of water flowing between some rocks and carried enough to the student in his hat.

In the meantime, the hotel guests waited in great anxiety, most of them on a meadow near the hotel from where a good view of the mountain slopes could be gained.

The "boots" carried an electric torch which he had agreed to flash when the student was found. The torch duly flashed: the student was found; but in what state? That was the question which now agitated his family and the hotel guests. The "boots" had agreed to yodel. A joyful yodel would indicate that the accident had not been serious; a melancholy yodel would signal a severe injury. No one, incidentally, thought this a strain on the "boots'" vocal chords. Finally a yodel was heard, but rather a mild kind of yodel which, in view of the distance, could have meant both bad and good news. The "boots" later explained that since the student was indeed injured, but not fatally, he had attempted something neutral.

We children were up early the next morning to see the return of the rescue party with the injured young man. As the little party approached the hotel, the student got off the stretcher and insisted on walking. He was supported on both sides, but he achieved a nonchalant air that was most impressive. His coat was torn, but a blanket was slung carelessly over his shoulder and he was smoking one of his favourite cigarettes. He showed complete indifference to the pain he must have been suffering, proving to himself, to his family, and to us that he was well worthy of his corps. He waved cheerfully to the crowd with his uninjured arm, pausing to permit his father to light a fresh cigarette, the father demonstrating great pride in being allowed to do something he would never be permitted to do under other circumstances.

At the time it made me think how funny are fathers, including my own father, with anything concerning their sons. I found later, when I was the father of a grown son, that I was not in any way different.

# CHAPTER XIX

IT HAD been arranged long before we left for Ammerwald that, after a time there, I should leave the family party, now that I was growing up, and go for a walking tour with that friend, one of father's guests at the hotel, who had joined me in the attempt to reach the injured student on the Vulture's Head. When first arranged, this tour had promised to be delightful and hitherto I had always enjoyed similar trips immensely; but when the time came to start, I did not want to go. I wanted to stay with the family at Ammerwald. I do not think the family were deceived into thinking this hesitation an excess of devotion to them. They knew I was in love again, and more seriously than usual, now with one of the student's sisters.

That South German manager and his family were devoted to England and everything English. I expect they really meant Britain and everything British. To say they were Anglophile would not be enough; it would be almost true to say that they suffered from Anglomania. When the student son wanted to praise the beauty of a girl he would invariably say that she recalled an English etching. When they played tennis only English tennis terms were used, no German word being tolerated. Everything English was wonderful and above criticism.

This attitude was definitely emphasized in the soul of the student's sister. She was near my age. She was devoted to the novels of Sir Walter Scott; and since Scott was one of my own favourite authors, we had much in common in dwelling on his romances and especially on the parts which dwelt on love interest. From this naturally flowed a delicious desire to be Walter Scott characters; and I soon felt not the slightest difficulty in seeing myself as the valiant and virtuous knight Ivanhoe, as I think the student's sister saw herself as the beautiful and virtuous Lady Rowena.

Soon we were deeply in love, holding hands whenever we could without being seen and exchanging letters of a highly sentimental kind. Always these letters ended with an entreaty that they should

be destroyed at once. We, my beloved and her beloved, saw ourselves on a much higher spiritual plane than the down-to-earth
one trodden by the other hotel guests in their commonplace love
affairs.

How could the knight Ivanhoe abandon the Lady Rowena to
go on a mere walking tour with a man friend?

The knight had no choice; the knight had no choice because
he would not have dared to give the reason why he felt the walking tour might be abandoned: and so, with his friend, he set out
most reluctantly one morning early. The friend felt equal reluctance: he was in love too, but I may not give away his secret.

The minor road from Ammerwald eventually reaches the main
arterial road between the Bavarian Highlands and the Austrian
Alps. The minor road was closed to motor traffic and, in those
days, people enjoying a walking tour even on main roads were
seldom disturbed by cars. But it happened that just at this time
the main road we eventually reached had been set apart as a
training course for the newly born motor-racing sport and, what
made everything worse, one of the first alpine car races was due
to begin within a few days. Competitors were now training,
hoping to gain as much experience as possible on the winding
road we proposed to follow for our peaceful walking tour. Monster
after monster, or so they seemed in those days, thundered by in
clouds of petrol fumes and terrific noise. Every few seconds we
had to jump for our lives.

There seemed many more cars than we thought existed in the
whole world in 1909. When we discovered that the racing cars
were following a wide circuit and that we were seeing the same
cars again and again, that, in consequence, there would be no
peace on that alpine road, we both turned about, without debate
or argument, and decided to go back to Ammerwald. We got
there before sunset and at once made it perfectly clear that we
had abandoned the walking tour simply because of the heavy
motor-car traffic. Our protestations on this point were received by
the younger people at the hotel with raised eyebrows and some
derisive smiles; but they seemed glad to have us back in the gay
community and father had no hesitation in extending his hospitality to my friend, who did not, as a matter of fact, stay with
us much longer.

Apart from anything else of a more tender nature, I was glad to be back, because much happened at Ammerwald which I was glad not to have missed.

For instance, I was there for the Emperor's birthday on the eighteenth of August, and it was a well-established tradition in Austria that this should be celebrated. The proprietors of hotels were expected to serve a particularly elaborate meal on the great day, to which they had no objection, apart from their national loyalty, since they enjoyed compensation in largely increased orders of wines and spirits. Tradition also demanded that the Austrian of highest rank present should propose the health of the old Emperor, any kind of refusal to accept this honour being out of the question.

Father narrowly escaped the honour through the presence in the hotel of an elderly *Hofrat* who had held, or perhaps still held so far as I know, a position of importance in one of the ministries. A long life spent in the company of deeds and documents had affected the skin of this old gentleman. It had become parchment, and those muscles of the human face used by ordinary people when they smile or laugh would not work any more for him through lack of use. There was evidence that he was human, but this was not obvious.

The company at the gala dinner was naturally very mixed. It included the gay *Postfraeulein,* who by now had shown all the grown-up males where the best beauty spots in the forest might be found. And there was the loquacious traveller in wall-paper who told little stories almost continuously, little stories with his wife as the stooge, much to her embarrassment, because she tended to be somewhat shy in company. A story beginning with "When my wife massages my back", or "When my wife rubs me down after a hot day", would see the frightened lady blushing in anticipation and hiding her face in her hands.

The *Hofrat* was, of course, sitting at the head of the table and when the right moment arrived and every guest had his glass full, he tapped his own glass with a spoon, and rose amidst applause. There was the usual dead silence. Father was intently watching the *Hofrat,* and I was watching father.

"I am very much annoyed," he began and then stopped suddenly before correcting himself, "no, no—I beg your pardon: I am very much *honoured* to have been chosen. . . ." And then followed the adulatory remarks usual on such occasions.

Father had difficulty in hiding his amusement at this slip of the tongue. Later he explained to us in the crystal-clear way he had when he explained anything, whether his own theories, architecture, or the life of animals and plants, that the *Hofrat*'s slip of the tongue in a psychoanalytical sense showed clearly that the elderly councillor did not really feel honoured; that he felt himself to be high above his company; that he, a senior civil servant, was indeed annoyed at having to address such people; and that his unconscious mind had made him tell the truth.

The student brother of my beloved was now back from hospital carrying his arm in a sling. He was much less haughty. I noticed this particularly when he asked me to play tennis with him, a very great honour I accepted without dwelling too much on the fact that I was quite the worst player within reach and the only opponent a man with one arm in a sling could take on. He was friendly and charming with no hint of his former haughty corps-student attitude to mortals. The transformation seemed to me miraculous, and I wondered if that desperately needed drink of water offered to him in the hat of the "boots" on the Vulture's Head had worked the miracle.

Towards the end of our stay at Ammerwald, and shortly before father left us to go to the United States, the status of Ammerwald changed dramatically from a quiet backwater holiday resort of middle-class people to an important shooting centre reserved for the highly privileged classes of those days.

There must be something exciting and entertaining in an arranged shoot if one may judge from the joy it apparently gives to otherwise kindly people; but to us its organization, as we saw it at Ammerwald, lacked any glory or even much interest. The hunters did not climb mountains to track and outwit the fleeing deer and thus to be on something like equal terms. The sportsmen sat in comfort on easily accessible points and the deer were driven past these points by a battalion of rangers and foresters. It was practically impossible for a hunter to miss his target. Still, shooting was taken very seriously in those days, giving the democratic Press and the caricaturists much ammunition.

The attitude of the Freud family was natural enough. We

were brought up in a peaceful atmosphere, and the killing of harmless animals for pleasure was alien to us. Father, as long as I knew him, never owned a weapon, not a gun, not a sword nor even a dagger; and I am sure he hated the dress sword he had to wear as part of the uniform of an officer in the medical corps.

I cannot say that my attitude was as peaceful as my father's in the years that followed. During the First World War I made a collection of booty swords and guns; and as a soldier I was concerned in killing other soldiers in the usual impersonal way. But when I was invited as an officer to shoot deer in a forest, and a beautiful roebuck appeared at a most convenient distance, I abondoned my rifle and offered the beast a biscuit.

There was a certain amount of pageantry at Ammerwald which was interesting. Our hotel became the headquarters of the Forestry Commission, and the highly noble sportsmen were the guests of the Prince-Regent of Bavaria. At the end of the day's shooting, they all met ceremonially in front of the hotel, a performance watched by us, including father, with interest but not deep-seated admiration.

We children were somewhat frustrated in our view of the ceremony by the women's hats, then as big and clumsy as millstones and, what made everything worse, the ladies naturally stood in the front row. When there appeared a tall, dignified man to whom the rangers and foresters showed deep respect, we asked father if this were the Prince-Regent? He appeared to us quite advanced in years and, consequently, it seemed certain that he was the Prince-Regent. He was, in fact, sixty-four.

"No," whispered father; "that's his son," which astonished us. How could a son be so very old?

Next came a sedan-chair and sitting in this was a very old man. This was the Prince-Regent. It was whispered in the crowd that he was eighty-eight, but he looked twenty years older. Nevertheless, he appeared to be alert and his expression was most friendly as he got out of the chair and began distributing cigars to the foresters and rangers. Clearly he was a kind and benevolent old man and there was no doubt that the forest personnel loved him. He immediately won the hearts of us children; all prejudice left us and we decided that he had not killed many, if any, of our lovely deer. The idea that those thickly veined and shaky hands could press a trigger seemed absurd.

When the killed deer were brought and laid out in a long row, we asked if we might go: we could not bear the sight of the deers' glossy eyes.

"Let's go, father," we suggested; "we've seen the son of the Prince-Regent and we've seen the Prince-Regent."

"Perhaps if we wait, we'll see *his* father," said father with a touch of malice.

# CHAPTER XX

THOSE happy days when something like a tribe—father, mother, six children, mother's sister and often father's brother as well—went on holiday: those happy days passed. Two sons left Vienna to study in Germany; two sisters married; father's brother, Uncle Alexander, married so that we saw much less of him; and then only a small circle remained—the parents, mother's sister and my youngest sister, Anna, who, as the years passed, became more and more indispensable to father. I myself remained in the Bergasse until 1914, when the First World War ended for us, as for so many, a period of freedom, prosperity and security.

One can only judge from one's own experience; but for people of my age the years before 1914 seem a golden age, a time when one could live in tranquillity and peace. Nothing like those years has returned for us. But even as I write these words and look back on those days I am bound to ask myself whether or not I took advantage of this tranquillity. I think not; and I become more convinced of this as I now browse through old papers and press cuttings, and as I look at old photographs and letters. It is clear that I had no talent for tranquillity or any particular love for a peaceful life. I was always getting myself into some kind of trouble and appearing in the daily press, astonishing it now seems for so completely an unimportant person. Sometimes my troubles were quite serious and, without father's protecting hand, anything might have happened to me.

In 1911 I had a serious ski-ing accident on the Schneeberg, every detail of which appeared in the Viennese press. In 1913 I was badly hurt in a brawl between German-Austrian and Jewish students, this case being made more interesting to the newspapers by the fact that the rector of the university, a famous medical man, gave me first-aid. A more serious incident occurred when at a public meeting I made a spirited attack against a crusade whose object was to abolish duelling. In the court proceedings that followed I was fined fifty kronen, but on this occasion father's

My mother with my son, Anton Walter, when he was an officer in
the Parachute Regiment

Two brothers—Sigmund and Alexander Freud

protecting hand was withheld: I had to pay the fine myself. I am not proud of this affair, for I have long since changed my mind and do not now think duels really necessary.

I had many adventures and indulged in plenty of escapades unknown to the press—duels, student brawls, and a considerable number of mountain rescues, some of which were successful. As a young man, neither tennis nor golf interested me; to my mind in those days any sport in which you could not kill yourself had no moral value. Thus, it may be suspected, the allegedly dreamy, peaceful days before 1914 had an exciting and occasionally a painful reality for some people of my age.

But I have to admit that despite this reckless attitude towards life, I was always very careful when responsible for the lives of others in climbing or ski-ing expeditions. I always brought them home alive. A friend of mine at this time was less successful or less careful; perhaps he was merely unlucky. As a voluntary guide to a mountain club he returned a number of times with a story but without his party. When he returned a third time during a few years' service with the embarrassing news that he was the sole survivor, the club decided to deny themselves of his services, a decision he accepted with great astonishment and hurt pride.

I think my most interesting mountain trip was made on skis one June to the highest peaks in the Adamello group on the borders of Austria, Italy and Switzerland, a district which was at that time virgin and never before attempted on skis. We were a party of three, both my companions being students like myself, and each of us carried a hundredweight of food and equipment. We lived largely on dried foods, like Arctic explorers. One day we shared a primitive alpine hut with two Italian mountaineers. They had decided to cook for their meal a piece of raw meat which they had carried in a rucksack for several days exposed to the fierce rays of the sun. The meat was, in consequence, not beyond reproach. However, they grilled it over the spirit stove and put it on the table. They both concentrated their gaze on the meat for some moments without making a move to eat it. At last the older mountaineer turned to the younger and said, "Coraggio, Casimiro!" and carved himself the first helping.

Eventually I left my friends and made my way down the beautiful Val di Genova, back to the haunts of men. Having been heavily laden with food, ski-ing equipment and alpine gear, I had not had room for much toilet gear nor for any change of under-clothing. Thus, unshaven, my face and neck covered with sunburn sores and my shirt in a frightful condition, I was not an attractive picture. I was joined on the road by a real tramp, who looked quite neat and tidy compared with myself. When he claimed me as a brother, letting me understand that all tramps should stick together, I thought it best to hurry on at a quick pace, the tramp shouting after me some remarks which I did not understand but which were not, I think, complimentary.

Of my many mountain adventures, I think the most dangerous and the saddest was one on Monte Cristallo. One of the friends of the Adamello ski-ing trip was lost on Monte Cristallo and his relatives telegraphed asking me to come to organize a search. His father, a very rich man, the president of one of Vienna's more important banks, had ordered that no expense should be spared and he sent his secretary to arrange with me the financial details. I led a large party of local guides to where it was assumed my friend had left the glacier to climb up an ice-covered rock wall. We found the place where he had fallen. His ice-axe, which I recognized, remained plunged deep into the ice. Very cautiously, we followed the direction of his fall, finding on the way his ruck-sack and boots which, as is usual in such accidents, had been torn from his feet. It seemed obvious that we would find his body in one of the numerous crevasses in the glacier. I, being the lightest and thinnest of the party, was lowered down into half a dozen crevasses, but there was no sign of the body. And yet had we known it, while we searched so carefully, he was, in fact, lying near us covered with snow. In late summer, when the snow had melted, his body was found perfectly preserved.

The loss of this friend was a great blow to me. We both shared the same enthusiasm for alpine climbing, a powerful cement in any friendship and strengthened where there is common respect. The father of this friend was, as I have said, a very rich man, so that money meant little to his son; but no member of any of our expeditions could have been more modest, nor more spartan than he was. Always he insisted on booking the cheapest accommoda-tion available, the *Matratzenlager*, communal sleeping-quarters where one slept on mattresses placed on the floor. It was said that on one occasion when he was forced to accept a room with a bed, he took off the mattress, placed it on the floor, and slept there as being more in keeping with the rules of true mountaineering.

To conclude this mountaineering digression, which has taken me away from my father and family, I might mention here that the secretary of my friend's father became, a few years later, the father of the famous film star, Hedy Lamarr. I can now boast that one day, when I was on leave during the First World War, I held an entirely unclothed Hedy in my arms. She was then two years old.

# CHAPTER XXI

FATHER had no difficulty in deciding what professions my two younger brothers should follow. They had, in effect, decided themselves. One showed a marked talent for architecture and the other was devoted to mathematical engineering.

I was the problem. I had not the slightest interest in, nor understanding of, my brothers' subjects. Medicine as a profession for any of his sons was strictly banned by father: which did not disturb me, even if there had been the slightest possibility of my going against his wishes. There remained law, but no decision had been reached when I became a student at a commercial college, the Export Academy, not against father's wishes, but without his enthusiastic support.

It has never been clear to me why I joined the academy, although I may have been influenced by the fact that a former student, by virtue of his training, was able to trade in Arabia and Syria, living there like a prince and becoming very rich. Perhaps the fact that Uncle Alexander had been a professor at this academy influenced me. I do not think I was affected by the fact that the Export Academy was in the Bergasse, opposite our flat, and very handy if one wanted to nip across during ten-minute breaks to enjoy a snack in our kitchen.

As it happened, I soon reached the conclusion, whether rightly or wrongly, that study of commerce as such is futile. My father thought this, but he had preferred to let me find out for myself. I think one is born with a capacity for business or one is not: and most certainly I was not. Several of our friends, grandfathers when I entered the Export Academy, had made great fortunes in commerce; but they had not been students at any export academy. They had staggered into Vienna from the provinces with one pair of shoes, if they were lucky, and two gulden (about four shillings) in the pockets of their frayed trousers. A commercial college can teach one book-keeping and certain business technicalities; but it cannot produce that flair which makes for success in business. Austria had no colonies; I had no relations in the export trade to give me a start, and it seemed clear that the end of my studies would see me an underpaid clerk in one of the Austrian export firms.

When father saw that I agreed with him, he suggested that I should study law. He had no difficulty in persuading me, the result being that during this first year I was registered as a student of both law and commerce, father having to pay the fees for both during the first year.

The first year's study of law in Austria in those days was concerned entirely with Roman law, old German law, and the law of the Catholic Church, the two last-named contending with each other in dullness. It began to dawn on me that I would not succeed as a lawyer and I became discouraged. I went to father for consolation, something he was always willing to offer, no matter how deeply he might be preoccupied with his own work. We had a long talk in his study.

He held the legal profession in high esteem, I think chiefly because those lawyers with whom he had become intimate were men of the highest moral and professional standards. It had always been his hope that one of his sons would become a lawyer. Thus he watched, and I think guided, my first faltering steps in my law studies with the greatest concern.

He agreed that my first studies were dull and boring, but he assured me that one day I would find a teacher with an impressive personality, perhaps a man of genius, and that I would become deeply interested and carried away by his lectures. Thus I would find happiness in my studies.

Father always expressed himself with great clarity and, when advising me at so critical a time in my life, he added to his normal clarity of expression a natural tenderness and concern entirely free from any kind of sentimentality. In a sense he was perhaps rather too successful in dealing with a subjective, or receptive, character like mine. Thus the teacher of impressive personality and genius, the shepherd who would lead me into green pastures of less boring and tedious mental nurture, assumed reality. He was waiting for me and it was only a matter of finding him as quickly as possible.

What I thought might be a short cut the day after the discussion with father led me at once to the largest lecture-room in the university, where the most famous expert on Roman law lectured. Here I took a seat in the third row, the nearest I had ever been to a professor. The gentleman came in and took his stance on the rostrum and began. I took notes with energy, the least I could possibly do as a newly born lamb in this old shepherd's flock; but I admit to surprise when I noticed that no one else was taking notes. The professor seemed rather too old to be a vessel of impressive personality; but you can never tell from exteriors and it was up to me to give him undivided attention. I was still under the influence of what father had said and remained looking for a sign or a revelation, something brilliant and fascinating. Still under this influence I found myself looking up at the old gentleman and, what was embarrassing, the old professor was looking straight down at me: possibly for only a second or two, although it seemed a long time.

I have not inherited any of my father's knowledge of the human mind, but possibly a tiny scrap of his faculty has come down to me as a kind of consolation prize. When anybody looks into my eyes, I can read what he thinks of me. In the ordinary way, this has never added much to my opinion of myself; but later, in law proceedings, I found this sixth sense invaluable. I began reading the professor.

"What is it you want?" I read; "you, sitting in the third row with your notebook on your lap. What mischief are you up to, sitting there and staring at me? I haven't been stared at for years. Why are you not peacefully sleeping like the other students?"

I soon found out that the professor had been delivering the same lecture for upwards of fifty years without changing a word. His lectures had been taken down in shorthand and copied so often that they had become the cheapest lecture scripts on sale, especially second-hand. They could be bought for little more than the cost of the paper. No wonder no one worried to take notes.

A number of years had to pass before father's prophecy was fulfilled, at least in part.

A more exciting incident occurred one day when I found the entrance to the university cordoned off by the police. No one was allowed to enter. The Austrian police, incidentally, were not allowed to enter the university, not even to stop such a fight as now appeared to be raging within its gates. Judging from the anti-Semitic shouts that could be heard, the battle was between German-Austrian students and their Jewish colleagues. What seemed remarkable to me was that the Jews were fighting back, and fiercely too: and this seemed to me out of character, possibly the first time in two thousand years that Jews, accustomed to being beaten up and persecuted, had decided to stand up for themselves. I felt I was witnessing an historic occasion.

The entrance from the pavement, where the police waited on guard, was formed by two broad sloping approaches and each had balustrades.

The Jewish students, I could see, were outnumbered by at least five to one and soon they were being slowly forced down the sloping approaches, both parties fighting fiercely with their fists and sticks. As I watched, I saw the German students concentrating their attention on one Jew, an enormous young man who had the strength of half a dozen of his enemies. They were throwing themselves at him and hanging on his neck.

The balustrades were apparently not too strong because, at a critical moment, one gave way, and the big young man and his assailants, in a whirling mass of caps, socks, sticks, cement and bodies, landed in the street. As it happened, the big young man came out of it very well because he had so many foreign bodies clinging around him that his fall was cushioned.

Since it may be wondered why socks were whirling about, I had better explain what I was told. Both parties in the battle tried to protect their skulls from the blows of heavy sticks by packing their caps, or hats, with their oldest socks, thus giving their hats the efficiency of crash-helmets. A brain has importance to a student.

The pavement outside the university was not academic territory, and so the police could intervene. This promptly ended the battle, the combatants dispersing quickly and the whole affair being ended, at least for the time being.

The idea that Jews might abandon meekness as a defence against humiliating attacks was new and attractive to me. A few evenings after the university battle, I went to the headquarters of the Jewish corporation whose members had taken part in it. There were a number of such corporations, but the one I approached, the Kadimah, was the oldest. The word *kadimah* means both forwards and eastwards. The members of the Kadimah were Zionists.

The Kadimah members I met that first evening appeared to my unsophisticated eyes to be strange and unusual men, entirely different in outlook and manners from the young men I usually mixed with. Without doubt, I in turn seemed the queerest fish that had ever wandered inadvertently into their net. Had I been a young female, they would have decided, judging from my manners and way of talking, that I had been educated in an exclusive convent. Nevertheless, they gave me a hearty welcome.

It was about dinner-time when I arrived and, when they discovered that I had not eaten, one of my future brothers took me to a little shop in the same block where an old Jewess sold gherkins and roast goose, cut into small portions, with chunks of black bread. We sat at a bare wooden table innocent of knives and forks and helped ourselves, eating with our fingers. I greatly admired a neighbour at the table who took in his fingers by the tail a large boned herring and slipped this down his throat. A tame seal could not have done better.

The members of the Kadimah came from all parts of the large Austrian Empire as well as from neighbouring countries like Serbia and even from the Caucasus, the result being that when the First World War broke out these foreign members had to serve with Austria's enemies. The most exotic member I met was that gigantic young man I had seen set upon by the German students in the university battle. He came from Turkestan. He had been one of three brothers actually enrolled by the founder and leader of Zionism, Theodor Herzl, who had met them during his travels. Two of these young men had left when I joined.

I had a most enjoyable evening and reached my home very late. Our apartment was so awkwardly arranged that father had to pass through my room on the way from his study to his bedroom. Since he never went to bed before the small hours of the morning, I was nearly always asleep when he passed; but now I was still up and glad on this occasion because I wanted to tell him about the Kadimah. Not that I was sure he would be pleased: Jewish citizens in distinguished positions had a strong prejudice against Zionism and, so far as I knew, he might easily regard my joining this club with disapproval, as another of the pranks that would run me into trouble and danger.

As it turned out, he was plainly delighted, and said so; and I may say now that many years later he himself became an honorary member of the Kadimah.

I have never regretted joining the Kadimah; indeed, I am still a member of the brotherhood which, owing to the Nazis, has been scattered throughout the world even as far as Australia. Members meet occasionally to recall old student days.

My success as a new member of the brotherhood was not as great as I could have wished. Being tall, slim and strong, it was confidently hoped that I would become a champion sabre-fencer; but the best I could offer was something rather mediocre. In any case, to my great disappointment, this had ceased to be important. I had, in fact, joined in the hope of opportunities to teach better manners to those who thought it excellent sport to humiliate and insult Jewish students, girl students not excepted. This was years before Hitler came to power, when Nazism as a name was unknown; but it was, nevertheless, the Nazi spirit in German-Austrian students that often made life so difficult for Jewish students. A year or two before I joined the Kadimah a meeting at the small and pleasant town of Waidhofen had decided that since "Jews were bare of honour" no reputable German student should allow them *ritterliche Satisfaction*, chivalrous satisfaction. This resolution was passed after a long series of victories won by Jewish over German students.

In my student days, when the resolution passed at Waidhofen was still fairly new, the Jews thought of a counter-move. It was decided that when the usual two German students arrived at the meeting where duels were arranged and one began, "We are sorry, but our principal feels bound to obey the rule established at Waidhofen——" a Jewish student with the biggest and heaviest hand should slap his face with all the strength at his command. Because my hands are slim and light for my size, I was never chosen for this job. Actually, the plan only worked with the element of surprise. The student bold enough to offer this insulting explanation soon learnt to find defence on the right side of a marble-topped café table piled high with dishes.

Thus I had no opportunity to fight these incipient Nazis under equal conditions, man to man. I had to content myself with joining in brawls when Jews were outnumbered by five to one, or even more. As I said earlier, I was wounded in such a brawl by a knife-thrust, and as I was the son of a university professor, the newspapers reported the incident with a wealth of detail. I remember when I got home that night, neatly and expertly bandaged, the family were at dinner with a guest, the Reverend Oscar Pfister from Zürich. I apologized for my appearance and father threw me a sympathetic glance. The clergyman, however, got up and approached me to shake hands warmly, congratulating me on being wounded in so just and noble a cause. This sympathy and kindliness from a dignified leader of the Christian Church heartened me considerably, making me feel less like a battered ruffian.

I fought two duels of the ordinary kind and they remain interesting, less for their causes than for the fact that I met both of my opponents later in life under curious circumstances. One of my opponents was a very big man and the other was a very small man. In both cases there were no miracles: in both, Goliaths slaughtered Davids.

I found myself years later sharing a small prisoner-of-war camp on the Italian Riviera with the Goliath who had slaughtered me. We were both Austrian officers living more or less on parole. Goliath had grown even bigger, so big, in fact, that in the melodramas we produced he was invariably chosen to be the executioner, with his mighty torso bare, masked and armed with a fearful-looking papier mâché axe. We became good friends, but my sixth sense was never explicit so far as his liking for me was concerned. Through father's generosity and his international connections, I was well provided with money and was one of the very few prisoners able and willing to buy drinks for a friend.

My meeting with the small man, the David whom I, as Goliath, had slaughtered, was even more strange. We were both refugees in Britain, and since forty-six years had passed since our meeting sabre in hand, we were both past middle-age. Both were what might be called self-employed. He owned a small café in London into which I often dropped on Sundays. He did not recognize me, but I knew him by certain marked mannerisms in his speech and movements. I could not remember his name, but

I did recall the name of his home town. To make sure I was not mistaken, I asked him one day what part of Austria he came from. He was the David I had slaughtered.

However, not for the world would I have embarrassed him by recalling our last meeting, contenting myself with spirited discussions on *Nusskipfel*, a crescent-shaped cake filled with powdered groundnuts, which he baked expertly and I ate with equal zest.

# CHAPTER XXII

HAVING been found fit for military service, I had to serve a year with the Austrian army. Students, in contrast to the three years others less fortunate had to serve with the colours, were let off with a single year; and we had another important privilege: we could choose the arm of the service we preferred. If left to myself, I would have chosen the cavalry because a number of my friends, called up earlier, were now hussars who could wear handsome uniforms, ride spirited horses, and win the attention of girls.

But father objected firmly to my choosing the cavalry and I had, in consequence, to abandon the idea. Since the days of Lavarone I had despised the infantry, the so-called Foot-rag Indians; and since father would never force me to do anything I disliked, there remained the artillery, a happy compromise, to which father agreed since he thought the artillery much less corrupt than the cavalry. The artillery was only slightly less expensive, because a so-called volunteer in the Austrian army had to pay for his horse, its saddlery and upkeep. Father, from his own experience, knew much about the Austrian army.

At this time, few guessed that a world war was only a few years away and that the game of playing soldiers in beautifully cut uniforms and immaculate boots would eventually turn into a bitter reality of dirt, hunger, wounds, epidemics and, for many officers, a soldier's grave on foreign soil.

If I may digress and look ahead for a moment, I might say that it turned out to be a good thing that father had forbidden my joining a cavalry regiment. As everybody knows, the war had not been raging long before it was decisively proved that the cavalry had ceased to be effective against what were then modern weapons. The Austrian mounted troops were particularly unlucky in that they soon lost most of their officers and nearly all their horses. The question of employing the survivors became a problem which was partially solved by putting them in military offices at home and abroad. Two of my hussar friends had survived and found themselves in an office under the command of an elderly colonel who had been dug out from retirement. The office was concerned with army supplies, and the Colonel made it a rule to interview personally every caller. Because dealings with the Austrian army were highly profitable to civilian merchants, the Colonel's ante-room was naturally always crowded with eager gentlemen waiting to be called to the Colonel's office. My two ex-hussar friends, both good-looking, both fair-haired with blue eyes, sat calmly at their desks throughout each day in their gold-braided uniforms, presumably as secretaries or receptionists, and doing little or nothing whatever.

One day the Colonel, armed with a visiting-card brought to him by an orderly, went to the ante-room, as was his habit, to look over the caller as a preliminary move before leading him to his sanctum which he shared with my two friends. He returned alone in some excitement to say, "Listen, my lads: let this be a lesson to you! The fellow who sent in his card was a Jew. He wanted to see *me*. Well, I expect you can guess what happened: I threw him out." Then, raising his voice, the old fellow went on, "So long as I am in command here, no Jew will ever enter this room."

Both my friends were Jews, and highly amused Jews at that moment, even tactful Jews who succeeded in hiding their grins.

My service in the Imperial Horse Artillery began in 1910 when I was nineteen years old. Mother, who had much experience in looking after father's clothes, took a hand and ordered my uniforms from one of the better military tailors. They fitted beautifully. I had four different outfits, a great contrast to war days when I had one blouse and one pair of breeches, both several sizes too big, which I wore day and night. My parents saw no objection to the custom, followed by most of my comrades, of renting a room near the barracks. My landlady called my room a sleeping saloon, and I had an idea that in better days it had been the family's drawing-room. I was made most comfortable and since as a lodger I was never late in paying my rent, I won the reverence and respect of the good landlady who always addressed me as *Herr Einjaehrig Freiwilliger,* or, in English, Mister One-year-Volunteer.

Her knowledge of life as it was lived by Messrs One-year-Volunteers was greater than mine. One morning when I told her that I expected a lady visitor that afternoon, confidently expecting her to offer to bring coffee to the room, I was somewhat shocked when she promptly replied, "Very well, Herr Einjaehrig Frei-williger, I shall change the bed-sheets and pillow."

# CHAPTER XXIII

W E ALL agreed when I began serving my military term that the Austrian officer concerned with our training most certainly overdid discipline. There was hardly one of us who did not feel a certain amount of terror when this tyrant's steel-blue eyes were focused on him. He appeared to enjoy punishing young and ignorant soldiers, although the varying degrees of what appeared to be medieval torture still surviving in the Austrian army were not inflicted on those who, like myself, were being trained for future commissioned rank. We were given black marks instead, and these seriously affected promotion.

One chilly autumn day, the greater part of the Viennese garrison was paraded for an inspection by the Emperor. This, always a dreaded event, must have cost our troop commanders many sleepless nights as by endless drill they prepared us. As invariably happens there was, when the great day dawned, a long wait of upwards of four hours on the parade ground before the arrival of His Imperial Majesty: and then it was all over in a few minutes.

I could not see much of the Emperor because I was in a rear rank and the horse-tail-crowned shako worn by the tall man in front of me blocked my view. But I enjoyed an excellent view of roughly one-half of our tyrannical commander. I could see him plainly from his belt down to his brilliantly polished boots. I am certain that his head, neck and chest remained as rigid as stone when the Emperor drew near; but, much to the malicious joy of his pupils, who so often trembled before his stern gaze, his knees began shaking, not violently but in a sufficiently obvious manner.

Two or three months after the beginning of my military service, I got into a scrape which, I think, caused father some anxiety and worried me considerably at the time. It was called an affair of honour, but there was little honour in it. One morning in riding school, I was startled to discover that I had not brought my riding stick, a wooden rod used in training instead of the sabre which, to say the least, could damage a horse's ears if not used expertly. We usually carried these stuck in our boots when dismounted. Without thinking, and without waiting to ask permission, doing something not unusual amongst us, I borrowed a riding stick from a man standing near who had completed his morning's drill. I had chosen badly; this fellow was bad-tempered and disagreeable; and the result was that he promptly punched me. I returned the blow with interest, following this up by flinging the stick in his face.

Thus I was again without a stick and risked delaying the beginning of my squadron's exercise. Fortunately for me, a friend, seeing my dilemma, broke ranks and handed me his stick, and I was saved for the moment. I was in so great a hurry to mount my horse and to join my squadron that I do not think I thanked this thoughtful friend. And since, as I now contemplate this event with, perhaps, more gratitude than I felt then, I wonder if I ever did thank him. He, Baron Josef (called Pepi) Schenk, may read this book if he is still alive. If he does, I can now say, "Will you, Baron, accept my belated thanks?"

Unfortunately, that was not the end of the incident. There had been at least sixty witnesses, including the officer in command of riding; and it was clear that a scuffle between potential officers could not be overlooked. My adversary was the son of an important general, but this did not prevent him taking a decidedly one-sided view of the incident, a view in which I was the sole culprit: a dangerous view if shared by authority, which could have ended in my expulsion and disgrace. I overheard him urging one of the sixty witnesses to agree with this, but fortunately for me, he chose a decent, honest man incapable of lying.

Nevertheless, the fellow made some progress. I saw the light when people around me, including the junior officers, began treating me, not unkindly, as a condemned man.

The only thing to do, I now saw, was to talk the matter over with father. Fortunately, I had not been confined to barracks.

There was no need to explain to father the spirit of the Imperial army: he knew more about it than I did. He took a serious view of my position and determined to set in motion a counter-influence. Professor Koenigstein had a son-in-law who was an army medical officer, only of captain's rank, but one who had won by his charm

My father resting in the garden

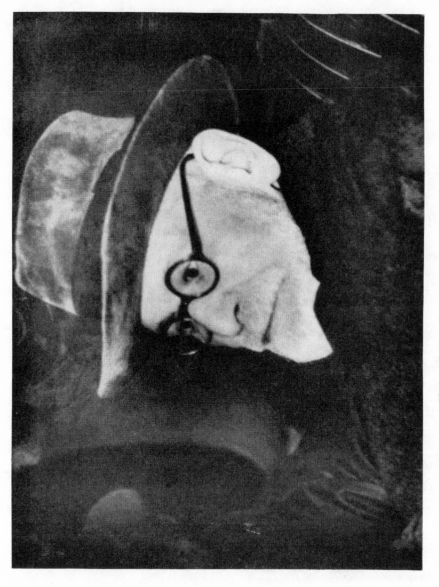

Sigmund Freud arrives in London, 1938

and ability many influential army friends. He was a Jew, incidentally; but since most Austrian army medical officers were Jews, his faith did not in any way affect his popularity. He was very much a friend of our family. I can still recall mother reorganizing the sleeping accommodation in our summer holiday villa at Aussee when this officer arranged to spend a day or two of his honeymoon with us. The best room in the house had to be made ready for the young couple.

By a lucky chance, one of this medical officer's best friends was a general with whom he played cards regularly, a bond of great importance, as important as a golf partnership in Britain and America today. The General happened to be the officer who, amongst other duties, supervised the officers' training schools in Vienna. Thus I had the doubtful honour of being singled out by this great man during one of our lessons and asked a number of questions designed, I am sure, less to test my military knowledge than to find out what kind of a soldier I was. To oblige a friend, the General had decided to intervene, but it was important to find out what kind of creature he had to save.

Evidently, I passed the test; the atmosphere soon changed and in time the riding-school incident was resolved, very much against army regulations, by mutual apologies.

Another so-called one-year volunteer was less fortunate. At a fashionable spa on one of the beautiful warm Carinthian lakes, where young, rich and careless Viennese met together to play in the warm sunshine of July days and the even more seductive, or treacherous, moonlit nights—at this fashionable resort there appeared a young girl, the daughter of a successful merchant who had been recently knighted. She was very young and very gay, and if she was not particularly pretty, she was not plain. She loved music and dancing and handsome young men. Perhaps she was a little too normal; she had no inhibitions.

Unintentionally, perhaps unconsciously, she seduced every young man she liked; or perhaps it is truer to say that she met every advance from a young man more than half-way. Since not all young men are discreet, she soon won a reputation which made it easy for her to find partners.

A few months after the holiday was over, the girl had to confess to her parents that she was an expectant mother. Her father, who, unlike everybody else at the spa, had had no idea what had been going on, became delirious with fury and his hate naturally concentrated itself on the villain who had seduced his innocent child.

"Who was it? Who was it? Tell me his name!" he shouted again and again.

The unhappy girl was at a loss. She dared not offer her angry father a long alphabetical list of young men and then go on to explain that it must have been one of these. To quieten her father's raging, she had to choose one from the list, and since it would not have been wise to settle on the least attractive, she decided on the best-looking and, incidentally, the most gentle, the son of good and highly respected parents.

That very old rule that the honour of a disgraced girl can be restored by marriage with her seducer could not be applied in this case. The boy flatly refused to marry her, and the code of honour forbade him to explain why. In consequence, the father's fury burnt even more brightly. Had he taken a gun and shot the alleged seducer of his daughter, society would not have blamed him. He succeeded in being much more cruel, in doing something without precedent: he went to the Emperor.

Since the father had been knighted but recently, the audience was not hard to gain; and because the Emperor, a cavalier of the old school, had not the slightest doubt that the female is always the victim and the male invariably the aggressor, he promised severe punishment.

The boy was expelled from the artillery officers' training school and sent to his regiment for three years as a gunner in the ranks, with directions from the highest authority that he should receive special treatment, a direction that made his survival unlikely.

# CHAPTER XXIV

M Y CAREER in the Imperial Artillery ended abruptly on medical grounds after a few months' service. This was the result of a ski-ing accident on the Schneeberg. It was customary at the school to grant all ranks a free week-end during the first week in January, and I took this chance to ski with two soldier friends.

They were both highly expert skiers, even champions, something I had not known, and I expect they were unaware that I was no better than good average. A man who has succeeded in driving straying cows from his garden will not necessarily succeed as a toreador in the bull-ring, and he would be silly to make the attempt. My desperate efforts to keep pace with my two friends that Sunday on the Schneeberg met with inevitable disaster: I fell and broke my leg, and sufficiently far from the alpine Hotel Hochschneeberg to make a rescue arduous.

The pain and discomfort of this accident are long forgotten, but the memory of the devotion and self-sacrifice shown by those boys remains fresh in my mind. One went for help, and the other remained with me until a small rescue party could arrive from the hotel.

Today, an accident would seem to be part of the fun of ski-ing, medical attendance being supplied locally with as much charm and efficiency as champagne at a gala dinner party. Only a few days ago my son, returning from a ski-ing holiday on the Arlberg, wrote to say that his train was like a hospital train, and, I would add, filled with happy and contented patients.

In 1911 there was little sympathy wasted on ski-ing victims and no degree of tenderness. When, after travelling all night, the stretcher carrying me reached the Hotel Hochschneeberg, it was deposited in a passage and I was left to the mercy of the hotel servants while the bearers hurried away to look after themselves. My two friends had had to leave for Vienna the night before to be in time for the Monday morning roll-call. When, after a few hours, I was able to attract attention, I asked the housekeeper why I had not been brought food and drink. She replied brusquely, "The gentleman has not ordered anything."

There was no one at the hotel able to give first-aid and my broken leg was left unsecured in any way until a doctor arrived with a friend of my family. Neither the doctor nor my friend could ski and they had had to make the ascent to the hotel, which was not far from the summit, on *Schnee-Reifen* (snow-shoes), a device which does prevent one's feet from sinking too deeply into snow but is an arduous way of getting along. They were both exhausted when they reached me. Conditions at the hotel being quite unsuitable for any kind of surgical attention to my leg, the doctor decided that I should be taken as soon as possible to a hospital in Vienna. My stretcher was therefore placed on a sledge and eight men towed me to the nearest railway station.

Although it was a week-day and, in consequence, there was plenty of room in the train, the conductor carefully calculated the number of seats my stretcher would replace and charged me for eight.

According to the rules, I should have been delivered to a military hospital. As I worked it out, I would have arrived at a military hospital shortly after the doctor's daily rounds. This would have meant a delay of twenty-four hours and, I should imagine, the amputation of my leg, possibly by one of the military doctor's assistants, who would thus be given a little training in major amputation. Fortunately, father had intervened and I awoke to full consciousness in a good private hospital where I was looked after efficiently. My leg was in a bad way. The men who carried me on a rough stretcher from the scene of the accident to the hotel had done their best, but often the broken leg had hung loosely over the side of the stretcher and thus the damage had been added to. My leg had swollen to twice its normal size and bits of my ski-ing trousers had become embedded in the wound.

Before my school Commandant could send out a patrol with fixed bayonets to arrest me, father called on the gentleman to explain everything. He had to wait on a shabby landing outside the Commandant's room while that officer dressed. First of all the batman entered the presence bearing a brown tunic with red cuffs and collar (the Commandant was a captain); then followed the sky-blue riding breeches and, finally, the beautifully polished jack-boots. In due course, all three reappeared with the Commandant inside them.

Father's apologies for my absence from duty were accepted with courtesy, the Commandant assuring him that this would be a final farewell to arms, that from then onwards the Austrian artillery would have to manage as best it could without his eldest son.

I cannot leave this incident without paying a further tribute to my ski-ing comrades. The one who stayed with me while the other went for help had two of his toes frozen. His name was Jaeger. He managed to catch the last train for Vienna by a fraction of a minute. Since to be absent at roll-call was an unthinkable crime, I asked him later what he would have done had he missed the train. He said that he would have ordered a special train: and this was no boast, because he came from a wealthy house and, as he said, he always carried enough money to meet such an emergency. His great wealth had no effect on his friendly simple character, but it did inspire the school Commandant to make him the school treasurer responsible for the collection of all contributions levied on the pupils, from chalk for the school blackboard to cough mixtures for the horses. During his term of office all dues were paid promptly, Jaeger meeting any deficits from his own pocket.

Jaeger was killed in action as an artillery observer in the First World War, and I am sure that the friendly smile, never long absent from his face, was there to meet the Russian bullet that ended his fine young life.

The three and a half years that followed my release from the army were spent in study for my profession, hard work relieved by mountain-climbing and ski-ing. This period was so entirely free of complications and problems that some persons in the still very small circle of psychoanalysts gave it as their decided opinion that I, an exception to all the rules, had no unconscious mind and not even a super-ego. Little as I knew of psychoanalysis, I nevertheless felt safe in accepting this as an insult.

I still lived in the small bed-sitting-room in the family flat in the Bergasse, sleeping on the same very old and hard horse-hair divan which I had occupied since boyhood; and father in the small hours still passed from his study to his bedroom. For some little time before my final law examination, instead of seeing me asleep, he found me with my nose in my law books.

"Overstraining your mind won't help, you know," he always said. "Take things more gently. You should be asleep at this hour."

For once, he was not convincing. An admonition, even a gentle one, could not be convincing from father, who had never spared himself.

To reward me for the successful completion of my studies and to celebrate my achieving the degree of doctor of law, father used his influence to the extent that I was able to choose the court in which to begin my legal apprenticeship. I chose Salzburg because I thought it the most beautiful town in Europe and within easy reach of magnificent mountain country.

It might be explained that in Austria, after one has passed one's law examinations, one serves for a full year at a law court as an unpaid legal apprentice. This is followed by six years as a lawyer's assistant at only a nominal salary. To survive seven years under these circumstances demands a wealthy and generous father.

I was still in Salzburg in August 1914 when the First World War began.

Time had brought many changes, and August 1914 saw our family dispersed. Father was in Karlsbad with mother taking a cure. My two elder sisters had married; my two brothers were studying in Germany, and Anna, the youngest, was in England. Unable to consult father, mother and the rest of the family, and impatient to be doing something, I promptly joined the army as a volunteer in my old regiment, the artillery. I was welcomed by the Battery Commander with a friendliness that recalled my first visit to the Kadimah. Nor was astonishment entirely absent from this warm greeting: the oldest inhabitant of Salzburg could not recall ever having heard of a man volunteering for war service after a war had started.

I might now describe the salute I helped to fire from the ramparts of the Hohen-Salzburg when we used cannon at least two hundred years old. I could write of the examinations at the Salzburg Training School which I passed successfully enough to become, for a number of days, virtually in command of it: sinking somewhat in a military sense when I was sent to the front as a corporal. Or I could describe father's visit to me at Innsbruck, a sad meeting because he appeared to be deeply depressed and far from well.

But it would be impossible here to say very much about my experiences in the First World War even if many stories by many soldiers of those days had not been told. I will confine myself to offering two or three translations of letters sent to me by father during my service, and I might attempt to describe some interesting days in the spring of 1915 when I served as a scout or mounted patrol in Poland.

# CHAPTER XXV

August 26th, 1914.
Dear Martin,

I have your documents including your release papers from the Court at Salzburg and I shall look after them for you. We now know that you have been moved, but not in which direction. We are hoping to have your Feldpost number so that we can send you what you may need.

The great news of the day is that Annerl [my sister Anna] arrived here surprisingly after ten days' journey via Gibraltar, Genoa, Pontebba, travelling with the Austrian Ambassador. She is very well and behaved bravely.

I hope you are well: you are playing your part in a good cause. I hope that you will write to us as often as you can. Some victories in Russia begin to appear more important together with the German victories.

Most cordial greetings——Your father.

My sister Anna was in England when war was declared.

Dear Martin,

First of all—congratulations on your "star"! Furthermore I had better tell you that I have sent you through my bankers two hundred kronen, which I hope will reach you. I do not think you need my advice about warm clothing, the importance of buying yourself some before you are sent away. I dreamt that I saw you in a thick fur-lined waistcoat. Frankly, so far as you are concerned, I am more afraid of epidemics, whose acquaintance can be made very easily just now, than of enemy bullets. It is not cowardice to protect oneself as far as possible from epidemics. I realize that correspondence between us will become much more difficult when once you have been sent to the front.

Cordial greetings——Your father.

A "star" in the Austrian army is equivalent to a stripe in the British and American armies. I might say that when the two hundred kronen duly arrived, I made father's dream come true by going to a furrier and having a fur-lined waistcoat made to measure. It kept me warm throughout the whole war and was stolen while I was a prisoner-of-war in Italy when, I expect, it could have done with some dry-cleaning. Also, I had some excellent boots made by the best mountain boot-maker in Salzburg, and these too lasted well. The regulation boots I was issued disintegrated when we marched through the snow to entrain. The soles dropped off, and I threw the remains through the window when the train started.

December 20th, 1914.

Dear Martin,

I am interested to hear that you are to be sent away very soon and I regret not being able to come to see you since you, yourself, will not be given any leave. I would not dare to make the journey just now while my digestive arrangements are so badly out of order.

I wish you well in your new unit; but I still think you regard the war as a kind of sporting excursion. I know that it is not safe to take with you anything you do not wear or cannot carry yourself: otherwise things are lost or immediately stolen. This is what we civilians understand from soldiers who have returned. For an officer everything is much better in this respect.

Let me know how much money you would like for the month of January. Do not forget that I will not be able to send you anything later: the Feldpost is notoriously unreliable. Nor must you forget that in Poland, or Serbia, you will have no opportunities to spend money. It is a matter of adjusting yourself to conditions that change momentarily.

Christmas will be quiet and sad here as everywhere. It will be sad and quiet with us.

I greet you cordially and look forward to your reply.

Your father.

I am aware that these samples of my father's letters to me can have little interest to those who merely know him as a name; they are not adorned with any expressions of affection and certainly not of sentiment. His letters were nearly always very much to the point and severely practical. Nevertheless, I knew full well that he was deeply concerned about the dangers he believed I was facing and the privations he was certain I was exposed to.

The truth is that I was then enjoying the happiest time of my life.

In the spring of 1915 victories had been won by the Austrian and German armies, and because of these we were able to advance into Russian Poland as quickly as soldiers could march. There was no mechanized transport in the Austrian army of 1915. The cavalry had been abandoned as a vital arm and the mobility of advancing troops was somewhat affected. There was no cavalry to fan out in front of our marching troops and each division had to improvise its own mounted patrols. My artillery unit was asked to supply a patrol rider and I was chosen, chiefly because I was twenty-eight pounds lighter than any one else who could ride and, in consequence, a suitable burden for a horse who would thus escape galls and saddle-sores even when forced to make long journeys. I had the advantage, too, of mountaineering experience and a consequent knowledge of map-reading which prevented me from getting lost often.

My orders were simple. I was to advance through no-man's-land in a north-westerly direction until I was shot at and then to pause until I had fixed my position on the map. After that my duty was to return to report. This was my work for many months, at first alone and later with an N.C.O. and two other ranks. I found patrolling more attractive when I was alone.

Sometimes a patrol would last two or three days, and then my orders were to ride only in daylight, to seek shelter by night wherever I could find it. My horse, a magnificent chestnut with a broad blaze, had been, like many other army horses, requisitioned and evidently he had come from superior stables. In England he would have been known at once as a first-class hunter. We soon developed a great friendship and I had every confidence that he would warn me of any danger. When forced to sleep in the open, I always chose the shelter of a tree in a meadow, and here I would sleep peacefully with my head on the saddle padding and the halter rope attached to an arm, the horse grazing around me and being very careful not to step on me.

There were few villages left standing, the Russians having scorched everything that might help their advancing enemy; but some out-of-the-way places had escaped. In one of these places I shared a peasant's hut with a small Austrian patrol and its owner, a peasant woman with a young daughter. There was only one room and only one bed which, in due course, was occupied by the woman and the pretty, playful daughter. We soldiers slept on the floor. Being on patrol, even the slightest undressing was dangerous, but on these occasions I risked removing the spur from my left boot so that I could cross my legs. Those who wore high boots had seldom much choice since, once put on, they remained on except when a man was wounded, when they were cut off.

It was a curious night. With several young soldiers in the bedroom so to speak, and young soldiers who were clearly attracted by the maiden, the good peasant woman felt bound to take what precautions she could. Like all peasant beds, hers was crowded with bulging feather mattresses and pillows. She built a kind of defensive works with these and put the daughter in the middle. If she had owned any needle and thread, I am sure she would have sewn up the girl as an added precaution, but needles and thread had vanished long ago.

The young girl thoroughly enjoyed the situation and when her mother fell asleep, she began peeping out between the feather fortifications and making friendly grimaces in the direction of the young soldiers. She was a nice, thoughtful girl evidently because, when she was certain she would not disturb her snoring mother, she began throwing out pillows, gifts that were gratefully accepted. She showed an unexpected sensibility by throwing me a particularly large pillow because she had noticed that I was tall and thin.

My father once said that true happiness comes only when a childhood's wish is fulfilled, the kind of dream-wish, one might call it, which most of us have as we build our castles in Spain. In one of my childhood's dream-wishes, I saw myself mounted on a magnificent war charger riding into a freed city to be welcomed with flowers and kisses from the liberated maidens, all very beautiful. Perhaps this wish is not uncommon with boys, if not so common as driving steam-engines. The reality, as it turned out, was even more colourful and the girls more lovely: and I was, indeed, completely happy.

It happened that, as the victorious Austrian army was marching towards Lublin, a patrol was called for to reconnoitre the city, to find out whether or not the retreating Russians had organized any delaying tactics there or perhaps had even arranged temporary resistance. Since the army was only about two days' marching distance from the city, I was sent out alone.

Trotting smartly along a dry pine-grove, I nearly collided with another horseman where pathways crossed. Since he was armed with a lance, I at first decided he was a Cossack and, with pistol drawn, I charged him with the hope of preventing him from getting his lance into position. Just in time, I discovered he was a German uhlan. Evidently there were others about and probably bound for Lublin with the intention of getting there first, a symptom of the uneasy partnership between Austria and Germany during the First World War. The greetings I exchanged with the uhlan were without friendliness.

As I went on with my patrol I was aware of my stupidity in mistaking the uhlan's mare for a Cossack pony. The Cossack pony was a lively, often temperamental but attractive beast, while the German uhlan mount, highly efficient and well trained, tended to be big-boned with rather a long head and the air of a strong-minded Prussian governess. Certainly it was easy for me to imagine the uhlan's mare in horn-rimmed spectacles sitting up at night in her stable knitting woollen comforts.

I pressed on with my patrol and I was, in fact, the first to enter Lublin. As I cantered up to the city's boundaries, I was met by a crowd of local civilians who had waited many hours for what they regarded as a happy event. Church bells began ringing and a company of pretty girls, in their traditional dress and carrying flowers, surrounded me. I promptly surrendered to their leader, a girl of fairy-like beauty who stood on her tiptoes near my charger ready to offer and to accept a kiss from the first Austrian soldier to enter the liberated city. Unfortunately, at this moment things went a little wrong through the well-meaning action of one of the other girls who, in her joy, threw a garland of flowers around the neck of my horse. Unused to such touching treatment, and already a little excited by the enthusiastic crowd, the horse bucked violently in an attempt to rid himself of the garland, and the result was that my kiss landed on the maiden's nose. Happily, steel helmets had not then been introduced; otherwise the poor girl might have suffered a severe bump on her forehead.

It had, I learnt later, been arranged that each girl in turn would salute the first soldier to enter the town, but when they saw how easily this tender salutation could end in a black eye, they contented themselves with blowing kisses through their fingers. Incidentally, my good horse, who was also a wise soldier, quickly reconciled himself to these reception ceremonies when the girls began feeding him with white bread. He was much luckier than his master in this respect. I had not tasted white bread for months, but I felt it would not be in keeping with the dignity and happiness of the reception if I had asked them to spare a little for me.

When, a day or two later, my artillery unit reached Lublin, I learnt that I had been promoted ensign: that, in fact, I had been riding about as a mere cadet when I was a grander person with better pay and the capacity to draw more respect from N.C.O.s. When this became generally known, sergeant-majors and sergeants stopped me to offer congratulations. These were somewhat soured when one of them, unaware that I was a Jew, tried to engage me in friendly conversation about the local Jews, numerous in Lublin as in other Polish cities.

"You would not believe," he began, "the prices these criminals are charging our men for everything they buy. The best thing would be if all our gunners went into the Jewish quarters and bashed in their heads. Not all the gunners, Herr Faehnrich," he explained, "only those off duty."

Naturally, I showed little enthusiasm for the man's suggestion, but I contented myself by remarking that since none of us had had the chance to shop in Lublin before, we could hardly judge any rise in prices. He agreed politely, admitting that he saw my point of view; but, clearly, the bashing in or the not bashing in of Jewish heads had slight importance for him. And yet I knew him to be an excellent soldier, a typically broad-shouldered fine-looking man of his rank. I might remark that all the officers knew of my race. Yet this conversation with the sergeant-major affected me quite seriously at that time, ruining my day and damping the happiness which had still lingered on from the coming true of my childhood's dream-wish when I rode into Lublin as a conquering hero.

During all my life I have had many opportunities to meditate on anti-Semitism. What seemed so strange to me was that it existed most strongly in some of the small towns and villages in alpine Austria where the inhabitants had seldom if ever met a Jew. It may be recalled that shortly after Hitler assumed power in Austria, he issued orders designed to humiliate Jews. When these orders reached the alpine towns, the inhabitants were at a loss to know how to obey them. It was decided to send the following telegram: "Impossible to obey orders; please send Jews."

I sometimes wonder whether or not this traditional hatred of Jews, nourished as it is by legend and fairy-tales throughout the centuries, will die out: witches are not burnt any longer in civilized countries.

# CHAPTER XXVI

WHEN the great Austrian Empire disintegrated at the end of the First World War, its army, still deep in Italian territory, fell to pieces. The different nationalities—Czechs, Hungarians, Poles and others—formed themselves into independent bodies and, with their arms and equipment, marched off to their native countries to enjoy newly won freedom from Austrian domination. The German-speaking units remained where they were, awaiting orders from Vienna, orders that never came. Finally, surrounded by British and Italian troops and having been told that an armistice had been arranged, they submitted to disarmament. They were then marched off to captivity.

The process was, in fact, neither simple nor straightforward; army movements seldom are, or never seem to be so, under the best circumstances; but the confusion, inevitable in view of our nation's collapse, produced much that was sometimes tragic and occasionally comic for individual soldiers. I know that I, one of the victims of the downfall of an ancient empire, went through weeks and months of hair-raising adventures before, like a bad penny, I turned up at a small officers' prisoner-of-war camp on the Italian Riviera to enjoy an early spring in pleasant and comfortable surroundings.

I had not been able to send news to my home, the result being that for a number of months father, deeply anxious, spent much time frantically writing and cabling to every possible government office likely to know something of the fate of my unit. Disorganization was so great that he did not even receive replies. It was not until March 1919 that he received the first Red Cross card I was allowed to send, and his and my family's fears were allayed. A regular correspondence, confined to these cards, began. Father had some difficulty in adjusting his large and bold handwriting to the narrowly spaced few lines which were permitted, but towards the end of June, after mother had written to say she had just been through the first serious illness in her fifty-eight years of life, father was able to keep me informed of her gradual return to comparative health. He was also able to tell me that reconstruction in Austria had made little or no progress and that, in consequence, my absence had not so far affected my chances in life.

At last, in August 1919, I was released and returned to Vienna, no longer a tall thin young man but somewhat plump as the result of a diet of spaghetti and risotto. On the other hand, my usually fulsome and gay spirits had thinned out, drooping to something very low indeed.

Also, I was very poor. Some thousands of kronen I had saved during four years of service, together with extra war grants, were not enough to pay for the re-soling of one pair of civilian shoes. This inflation, so devastating to the foundations of middle-class life, was bad enough; but the sense of insecurity, caused by an absence of discipline which permitted the mob to get out of hand, was hardest to bear. At my return one could still hear hooligans fearlessly singing in the Vienna streets: "Who will now sweep the streets? The noble gentlemen with the golden stars will now sweep the streets." Ex-officers like myself found it wisest to wear a scarf over their golden stars or risk having them torn off, and not too gently.

In the hospitals, the charwomen who scrubbed the stairs received two or three times more pay than the surgeons performing the operations. You might set apart enough money in the morning to pay for a suit, only to find that by the afternoon it would only meet the cost of the waistcoat. The cost of a *Schinkensemmel* (ham sandwich) in Vienna would also meet the year's rent of a luxury flat or a first-class railway journey from one end of Austria to the other. Nothing was safe on a train during those crazy days. A leather strap or a curtain still surviving would be cut or ripped down and put in a passenger's pocket without any attempt to hide the theft.

Father had lost his savings, and what provision he had made for mother became valueless. Eventually, of course, the economic reconstruction of the Austrian rump allowed people to awaken from a nightmare of disorder and dissolution and to begin at least an adequate if not a secure way of life. Father took what steps he could to restore his finances and I, as his eldest son and in his confidence, was able to help and advise.

Austria's illness had been painful, but the convalescence,

curiously enough, seemed sweeter than uninterrupted health, filling all with joy and satisfaction. Gradually, more and more people could meet cravings for long-missed things. To some it would be food, the return of the *Wiener Schnitzel*, the *Sachertorte* and the *Apfelstrudel*; to others, a new frock of fine and durable material to be shown in a ballroom aglow with sparkling lights; to me, ski-ing, mountaineering and canoeing; and to father, the reappearance of patients from foreign countries who paid their fees in British sterling, in Dutch guilders and in dollars. The Austrian currency remained highly perishable goods for a long time, sometimes more perishable than fruit and vegetables. Father was thus able to put by some savings and so to secure the future of his well-loved wife.

Clearly it is quite out of the question in a book of this kind to give more than a hasty glance at the years between 1919 and 1938.

In 1923, father became aware for the first time of the disease, cancer of the palate, which was to cause his death sixteen years later, the beginning of a long chain of operations—some severe, others less severe—and continuous medical supervision. Travelling far from home was now out of the question; and so the family, so reduced in numbers, had to make the best of the friendly seasons by moving out each spring to some villa in the outer suburbs of Vienna and remaining there until the autumn.

I recall three of these villas as being particularly charming. Built on the hills bordering the Wienerwald before the war by wealthy people, some of whom had now become the Viennese new poor, people who were glad of some increase in their reduced incomes, these homes were most comfortable if a little old-fashioned. They each had large and beautiful gardens. The last villa father and mother took in Grinzing had a garden, large enough to be called a park, in which one could get lost; and it had a fine orchard which offered delicious early apricots. Where the park ended, vineyards began and stretched for many miles.

From this Grinzing villa one had a magnificent view over Vienna. The steep road leading from the city to the hills passed the house. Mother loved this particular view and liked to sit in one of the bow windows watching people approaching like black ants in the distance and gradually assuming human form as they drew near. She was always aware of my approach even while I still remained hardly bigger than a black ant. I suggested during one of my frequent visits that she must have been guessing, that without binoculars she could hardly identify me. Her reply was characteristic of her methodical and observant mind. "When," she explained, "these little ants reach a point where the road becomes notably steep, they slow down. If one, an exception, marches on as if there were no difference in the road's grading, I know it's you."

The parks and gardens of the villas were the delight of the family dogs. It is no criticism of the British way of life to suggest that a British family dog appears to be the most important member of the family. Nor would I, myself, dare to offer criticism at this time when, in my own small Highgate household, a Welsh corgi's appetite or loss of appetite, his amiable moods or signs of displeasure, and even what appear to be his fancies, control the lives of the inhabitants. My family, and father emphatically so, had unconsciously become dog-lovers. Yet neither father nor mother had kept dogs in their youth. In mother's case, Jewish practice, which tended to regard the dog as an unclean animal, made keeping one as a family friend unthinkable. In father's case, it was a matter of poverty: he never permitted himself to be affected by religious considerations.

It was Marie Bonaparte (the maiden name and *nom de plume* of the Princess George of Greece) who showed father what a delightful friend and companion a dog can be; but I will reserve what I have to say about the dearest friend of father's later years until the time comes when I can try to show just what a friend can be.

During the period of the summers spent in the outskirts of Vienna, father kept Chows, and my sister Anna favoured an Alsatian.

Jofi was father's favourite and never left him, not even when he treated patients. Then she would lie motionless near his desk, that desk adorned with its Greek and Egyptian antique statuettes, while he concentrated on the treatment of patients. He always claimed, and we must accept his word since there were never witnesses during analytical treatment, that he never had to look at his watch to decide when the hour's treatment should end.

When Jofi got up and yawned, he knew the hour was up: she was never late in announcing the end of a session, although father did admit that she was capable of an error of perhaps a minute, at the expense of the patient. The two young red Chows which appear in the photograph with father on the balcony of one of the villas died of the disease which at this time destroyed nearly every second puppy in Austria. No expense was spared and everything possible was done to save his pets. Their loss caused much grief.

Anna's Alsatian, Wolf—a name that fitted perfectly—was highly intelligent. Anna used to take him for a walk early every morning in the Prater, having no difficulty whatever with him since he was well trained and obedient; but one morning, a squad of soldiers exercising near by fired a blank salvo into the air which so frightened Wolf that, much to Anna's distress, he disappeared like a streak of lightning. Certain that he would sooner or later return to his mistress, to whom he was completely devoted, Anna searched in every direction as she called him; but at last, seriously distressed since there was no sign of him, she was forced to return home. Here she was cheerfully welcomed by Wolf. He had taken a taxi home.

According to the taxi-driver, Wolf had jumped into his cab and courteously resisted all efforts to remove him while, at the same time, raising his nose sufficiently high to permit the taximan to read his name and address on the medallion hanging from his collar. Wolf must have thought the man rather stupid in not immediately understanding what he meant. The address, "Professor Freud, Bergasse 19", was plainly written.

There was already some concern at the flat through Anna's unusually late return and, while Wolf was welcome, the family feared something unfortunate might have happened to his mistress. However, Wolf's fare had to be paid.

"Herr Professor," said the taximan, "for this passenger I have not switched on the taxi-meter."

He was not disappointed with the fare father gave him.

Our dogs had the freedom of the flat and met everybody who came, being quite selective, even judicious, in the receptions they offered. The whole family, including Paula, our faithful maid, showed considerable respect for this canine sensibility. When the dogs condescended to be stroked, the visitor enjoyed the best possible introduction. If Jofi, for instance, sniffed somewhat haughtily around the legs of a caller and then stalked off with a touch of ostentation, there was at once a strong suspicion that there was something wrong with that caller's character. Contemplating Jofi's selective qualities at this distance of years, I feel bound to admit that her judgement was most reliable.

From the moment my father became internationally famous, he was continuously photographed until the end of his life and the result distributed throughout the world. For these posed photographs he used what his children called his *Photographier Gesicht,* his photographing face, rather a stern, serious face which did not for a moment reflect his kindly and friendly nature, not severe and reserved, as the world must regard him if they judge him by posed photographs. Sigmund Freud was a very nice grandfather and his true nature is always shown when he is photographed with a grandchild or two.

However, I can recall one instance when a grandchild brought upon himself father's severe displeasure, with oblique thunderbolts thrown in the direction of the grandchild's father—in my direction, because it was my son, then about four years old, who was the centre of the storm.

It had become the custom for the greater part of my grandmother's descendants to meet at her flat on Sunday mornings— her children, her grandchildren and great-grandchildren. She had, incidentally, moved into a small flat in a much better district of Vienna where she was looked after by Dolfi, her youngest daughter.

I was there with my wife and young son one Sunday morning, my small daughter being then too young to be presented. Evidently, my boy, who already displayed great independence of character, found the company of so many older people rather boring and, without taking anybody into his confidence, he decided to explore the staircase and finally the street. There was so much in the street that could be inspected, studied and experimented with.

The street outside grandmother's flat was usually deserted by traffic on a Sunday morning and remained peacefully quiet. But on this morning I became suddenly aware that Sunday's usual peace was being disturbed by somebody's vain attempt to crank up a heavy motor-vehicle. Perhaps instinct, possibly some knowledge of my young son Walter's deep interest in machinery, made me ask myself, "Where is Walter?"

Without answering this question, and now fearing the worst, I rushed out of the flat and down the stairs to the street followed by a crowd of elderly ladies.

We arrived at the moment of Walter's triumph. After many trials, it appeared that he had at last succeeded in starting the engine of a heavy lorry, and I found him standing in triumph at his full height of about three feet and apparently expecting applause. Instead of applause, he was promptly deprived of his magnificent toy, carried upstairs and forced to listen to a full and hostile account of his shocking exploit given to father by all the aunts, all talking at once.

This babel of female voices increased father's mild displeasure to anger, the severe form of anger usually shown by men who normally have excellent control of their tempers.

Father said in effect that there was not the slightest sense in becoming attached to a boy who must sooner or later kill himself in dangerous escapades, varying his theme in conclusion with a few cutting remarks about parents who were unable to control their children. I think the aunts enjoyed this shocking incident in a sad and deeply prophetic way, but neither my wife nor I found it pleasant.

I am bound to add that in this case father's pessimistic prophecy proved to be wrong. It is true that it was only by a chain of miracles that young Walter survived an exciting and stormy boyhood; but by the time he was called upon to serve in a parachute regiment of His Britannic Majesty's army, he had settled down to be a rather serious and highly respectable young man. He was demobilized at the end of the last war as a major: which, his father dares to think, was a decided achievement for a boy who had begun his service as an enemy alien refugee.

# CHAPTER XXVII

BETWEEN the wars, Austria, where for centuries no one had dared to challenge authority with any hope of success, endured what amounted to two civil wars. Incidentally, neither seriously affected father, who was never molested and was able to carry on with his work, treating patients and teaching, so far as his illness permitted.

During the first civil war, that of 1927, when the Socialists, inspired by Communist influence, were at the throats of the Conservatives, who at this time appeared to have a strong leaning towards the new Nazi theories, the Freuds remained neutral. Unable to decide which was the lesser evil, we kept out of the struggle and were not hurt. However, apart from the tragedy of the event, it did have a certain amount of entertainment value for neutral observers like myself.

My wife with her two children being at Bled, that former Austrian spa on a beautiful lake which had now become part of the new state of Yugoslavia, and knowing that they were without news and were probably deeply anxious, I decided to join them. My own district being held by the Conservatives while the railway station was occupied by the Socialists, it meant crossing no-man's-land with the chance of accepting a bullet not really meant for a neutral husband on his way to reassure an anxious wife at Bled. I duly found myself under cross-fire near the Karlskirche, that famous and beautiful baroque church; but war experience having taught me how to dodge bullets, I was not greatly disturbed until I met a girl of about eighteen running the same risks as myself but with less aplomb. She was terrified. I cannot recall any girl holding my hand with greater passion as we ran across the devastated public park to the lines of the Reds.

The great railway station was a scene of indescribable confusion, very natural under the circumstances. Packed with passengers, not one of whom knew whether or not it would ever start, my train stood under steam at its platform. A man with a red arm-band seemed to be in charge of the proceedings, but in answer to the many questions he was asked by excited and somewhat panic-stricken passengers, he could only shout again and again, "I have been on duty for five hours. I want to be relieved. I demand to be relieved immediately. This is an outrage. You must know," he complained, "you must know that nobody can be on duty for five hours without being relieved."

The Red's undoubtedly anxious audience heard this *cri du cœur rouge* with complete detachment. The passengers' interest was closely concentrated on the train's departure, and they would not have cared had he been on duty for five years.

I found standing-room in the train, which eventually steamed out, probably on the engine-driver's initiative, leaving me with the impression that if this was a sample of Socialist military organization, the Socialists' chances of winning were small. In fact, they lost this little civil war.

Upon my return from what proved to be a delightful holiday at Bled, I found my train running into trouble some miles short of Vienna. When it was forced to stop, apparently to avoid derailment where the permanent way had been sabotaged, it became my duty to carry a sweet baby with golden hair, and an elegant suitcase, both the property of an attractive young baroness who was deeply grateful and whose charm and beauty made the baby and the heavy suitcase as light as thistledown.

Had father seen me, he would have remarked that in the same way that I had seemed to regard the war as an occasion for sport, so I was treating the civil war as a chance to enjoy pleasant philandering.

When the civil war was over, and father could take his dogs to the kennels where they enjoyed a second home in a district called Kagran on the north side of the Danube, the lady who ran the kennels told him a story characteristic of the Austrian spirit,which a civil war could not affect deeply. Her husband, a police staff-officer, commanded the Conservative troops on the south side of the Danube. The north side at this point was held by the Reds. The bridge between the contestants, the Reichsbruecke, had been left intact. When night fell, the warriors all returned to their flats or houses, leaving the bridge under the light control of sentries. The bridge was a long one since it spanned not only the

Danube but also a stretch of barren low-lying ground three times as wide as the river, this low-lying ground being reserved to receive flood waters during the yearly inundations.

One evening, when the lady's husband was returning home across the bridge and had reached its northerly end, he was challenged by two Red sentries. "Halt!" they shouted. "Who goes there?"

"Lieutenant Commander Huber," was the reply. "You know me: I live across in Kagran."

In any other civil war in any other country, the colonel would have been shot at once or taken prisoner, but not in Vienna. The Red soldiers looked at each other questioningly, one remarking, "Yes, it is Colonel Huber all right: he lives near my home. We must let him through. What would his woman say if he did not get home in time for dinner?"

The Red sentries lowered their carbines; but instead of using the conventional "Pass friend!" they compromised with "Pass Mister!" since he was not technically their friend at the moment.

The second civil war occurred in the summer of 1934. Hitler had but recently assumed power in Germany and the Nazis now tried to get Austria into their grip. Because Austria's army and police force had not yet been seriously undermined by Nazi conspiracy and intrigue, they failed this first time, and the failure gave father and his family another four years of freedom in our native land. The Freud family were anything but neutral during this second civil war: all our sympathies were with the Chancellor Dolfuss and his successor, Schuschnigg. As is well-known, the attempt to win Austria depended a good deal on the native partisans the Nazis supported and secretly armed, support that was withdrawn when Italy sent troops to the Austrian border to show her objection to any planned annexation of our country. Nazi circles later explained this withdrawal as a faulty estimation of Italian fighting qualities.

When I heard that the state funeral of the murdered Chancellor Dolfuss would begin at the Town Hall, I decided to attend. To go as a civilian would have meant being pushed around and probably turned away. In the uniform of an Austrian officer I could command consideration and everything might be made agreeable. Ex-officers, when they observed certain rules, were again allowed to wear uniform upon occasions; but it meant parading in uniform at the War Office,where military identity papers were issued.

I polished my medals and succeeded in finding the other parts of my old uniform, including gloves, cap, dress sword and other oddments; but when I attempted to put on my tunic, I found that it would not cover my chest by as much as ten inches. This impasse was met by going to the market for unwanted goods at the lower end of the Bergasse, where I found a well-preserved tunic which fitted me excellently. And so, dressing in a great hurry, and completing the medal decoration as I marched, I reached the War Office, where I was received by a young officer of my own rank who proceeded to fill in the necessary certificate. He was most friendly, using the familiar "Du" of all officers of equal rank in the old Austrian army. This friendliness permitted me to ask him what I really looked like in uniform.

"You look magnificent," he said, an appreciation which agreed with my own secret opinion and pleased me very much until he added,"The appearance of some of the reserve officers I have met today has turned my stomach." I was magnificent, only in comparison, I saw, as I began making my way down the broad ornamental stairs of the War Office, nearly coming to grief twice, once when my legs became entangled with my dress sword and again when my feet got mixed up with my spurs: thus barely avoiding disgrace in the eyes of the smart military set which had changed so much since I had been one of them.

Having driven in a taxi over the Ringstrasse, I arrived in good time for the funeral ceremony, being allowed through the cordon of police and troops surrounding the imposing Gothic building where the funeral service was to be held, and being honoured with the usual salute.

Few Viennese people attended the funeral. The majority of the Viennese population were now Socialists who had become hostile to the Dolfuss régime after their defeat in the first civil war. A fair proportion were Nazis who regretted that the coup designed to bring down the Government had failed. However, there were many foreign correspondents present taking the usual photographs for their papers. If some of these photographs survive, they may show a lonely artillery officer standing at the foot of the small coffin, one obviously not at ease in his unaccustomed high stiff collar.

The service was soon over and the coffin carried out with military honours. The cordon around the Town Hall marched off and now I stood isolated at the great entrance with only the foreign correspondents to keep me company. They were busy packing their equipment. I tried to get into conversation with one or two of them, hoping to see a foreign and detached view of Austria's chances of maintaining her independence, a subject dear to my heart; but they showed not the slightest inclination to say anything to one they probably took for a mere low-browed artillery lieutenant. I consoled myself with the thought that they would not have been able to enlighten me very much. I had to continue asking myself how long Austria would be able to defend her independence.

# CHAPTER XXVIII

THE end of the First World War saw Austria divorced from Hungary, shorn of much territory, and left with thousands of lawyers with little to do since trade and industry had been seriously affected. Turning my back for the time being on the law, I found employment in one of the newly founded banks existing on the gambling made possible by inflation. None of them could last long; and thus I changed my employers a number of times although I did gain some business experience. I might remark here that even solid and well-established banking houses were mortally wounded by the economic crisis, a number of these dying more peacefully than others in state-assisted liquidation. I reached the position of assistant manager in one before all possibility of employment in banking ceased. Father was nevertheless pleased during the assistant-managerial period and never failed to address me as such on the envelope when writing to me.

Finally, I succeeded in making a living by writing articles on economic subjects for newspapers in Austria and Germany, but this work did not offer much security. The introductory quotation father used for his history of the psychoanalytical movement, Fluctuat Nec Mergitur (It floats: it does not go under), applied very much to me. However, things nearly always adjust themselves if they do not destroy one.

The period of the world economic crisis in 1933 saw father's publishing press in serious difficulties. This firm, established in 1918 with the help of a generous donation, had lost money continuously, not only depriving father of all income from his writings, but also threatening to use up his savings. A crisis in the business side of the press risked the discrediting of psychoanalysis in the eyes of the world.

The manager of the press had great artistic talent. His deep devotion to his employer allowed his friends to regard him in an amiable light, but did not permit them to place much dependence on his business ability. Financial considerations were alien to him. If he needed money he borrowed it; when a debt became due he endeavoured to prolong it or borrowed from someone else to meet it. Father appreciated all this, but the man was dependent on him and all he would say was "Lass ihn machen!"—"Let him carry on." I have to admit that this man was almost touchingly endearing in some ways. I recall one day when father handed him a completed manuscript. Clasping the packages to his heart in joy and admiration he marched off in apparent trepidation as if carrying a fragile and well-loved baby. He probably kissed it when he had got round the corner and out of sight.

Something obviously had to be done; but it took a long time to persuade father to make a change and to appoint me as his manager. I found the business side of the press in a shocking state, and I doubt if it would ever have climbed to a sound business basis and avoided bankruptcy without the valuable help given by the International Psychoanalytical Association and its president, Dr Ernest Jones. As it turned out, the Nazis eventually had the doubtful privilege of taking over something of substance and value and then destroying it utterly.

The work, I found, was enormously interesting and rewarding and, what was a great advantage to me personally, it allowed me some time to devote to my legal profession. I had been admitted to the Bar Association of Vienna, and father agreed to my using the press office for legal work.

It might be imagined that life at Bergasse 19, presided over by an old professor and his old wife, the former suffering from an incurable disease, would be dull and even sad; but this was not so. When father was free from actual pain, it was gay and cheerful. It remains associated in my mind with smiles and happy faces. Family jokes were welcome, but one practical joke I attempted tended to misfire and still makes me feel uncomfortable when I think of it.

A man in Sigmund Freud's position is bombarded by much correspondence, and it was often heavy work to sort father's mail, which was sometimes addressed to the press and sometimes to Bergasse 19. The cranks and other queer correspondents generally chose the press, and I would carry their letters as well as the more important communications with me on my twice-daily calls on father to discuss business. Father dealt with everything speedily and efficiently. For some weeks there had arrived most regularly letters from a German whose note-paper boldly proclaimed him to be an "Astrologer and Psychoanalyst". The letters asked for a meeting to discuss matters of mutual scientific interest, and their phraseology clearly proclaimed a crank. Father's verdict before destroying each of this man's letters was, "No reply!"

Nevertheless the letters from the "Astrologer and Psychoanalyst" continued to arrive and to grow so much in urgency that I felt bound to advise father to send some kind of reply, signed by me as his secretary, regretting firmly that a meeting could not be arranged. But father was adamant: there should be no reply.

The "Astrologer and Psychoanalyst" became something of a joke, but, as it turned out, not quite so much of a joke as I had imagined when I got our printers to design a visiting-card boldly printed with the gentleman's name, address and profession. A theatrical hairdresser having turned me into a grizzly old gentleman with abundant grey hair and a long beard, I placed horn-rimmed spectacles on my nose and walked to Bergasse 19, no passer-by taking the slightest notice of me and thus allowing me to know that my disguise was perfect. Paula was in the plot and admitted me and, although we had not confided in the dogs, they accepted me without question and nearly ruined the joke forthwith by their normal display of friendliness.

Paula went before me with the card, and I arrived in time to hear father shout, "By all means keep that man out!"

"Herr Professor," I began in a voice well disguised by my thick beard, "between scientists there are certain rules of behaviour, even if they differ in their theories——"

This was as far as I got. As father leant back in his chair, giving the "Astrologer and Psychoanalyst" so furious a glare that I must have paled under my disguise, Anna, whom it is very difficult to deceive and who was probably helped by the friendly behaviour of the dogs, cried, "It is Martin, Papa!" and the tension eased in general laughter. Nevertheless, I must admit that when I had removed my disguise, I endured an anticlimax that was not pleasant. Father's furious glare, although not really meant for me, had shocked and shaken me.

One of my jobs at this time was to look after father's income-tax. Knowing that he would insist on accurate figures being given, I always made a full and true return, showing a sum which in Britain or the U.S.A. would not have been considered extra-ordinary in view of Sigmund Freud's eminence, but in Austria at this time, where most professional people were poor, the figures appeared staggering. On one occasion when I carried the returns to the income-tax inspector, a middle-aged gentleman with a face so German that he could easily have posed as an extra in a Nibelungen film, I was astonished to hear him remark after studying the figures, "With such a return, the old gentleman would not have enough money to live on." He thereupon replaced my total with one of his own calculation, reducing the former by two-thirds, the corrections being made neatly with a perfectly sharpened pencil.

I met this same inspector some years later when I called at his office to settle the financial affairs of some former clients. Vienna was now under Nazi rule, and my inspector wore on his lapel an out-sized swastika as well as a badge proclaiming him to be a Nazi of old standing. He was no longer friendly since it was far from his duty to show much consideration to non-Aryans, but on the whole he was not unhelpful. Perhaps I was wrong now to decide under this frigid treatment that his former consideration was, in effect, an act of sabotage against the Government: that he had then decided that it would be better for the Jew to keep the money than to let it get into the hands of Schuschnigg.

As the manager of the International Psychoanalytical Press, I met all who were connected with psychoanalysis, being always treated with much respect, a little because of my job and very much because I was the son of the famous and venerated founder and leader of the movement. I basked in this reflected light and thoroughly enjoyed a social distinction to which I had little claim in my own right.

It is now that I can say more about the best and dearest friend of father's last years—Marie Bonaparte, the *nom de plume*, as I have already explained, of a great lady who might not like being so described since the adjective is one that does not appeal to Her Royal Highness, Princess George of Greece and Denmark. But I do not use it in a regal sense. For she had most of father's chief characteristics—his courage, his sincerity, his essential goodness and kindliness and his inflexible devotion to scientific truth. In this sense the similarity of character was almost startling. It would be idle for me to ignore the fact of my father's world-wide eminence; but contemplating this friendship in a purely domestic and social light, one cannot avoid seeing something unusual in it. The Princess had spent her youth in luxurious surroundings; her friend was an elderly Jew who had been brought up in the least attractive of Viennese districts, the son of an impoverished family with no social claims whatever: and yet they were in every sense of the word congenial.

Under father's guidance, the Princess made psychoanalysis one of her main interests in life; under the influence of the Princess, Sigmund Freud became a commonplace dog-lover.

The Princess favoured Chows, highly individualistic characters who may not be everybody's cups of tea, and father preferred Chows. When Marie Bonaparte wrote a book about her favourite Chow, Topsy, father was so delighted with it that, helped by Anna, he translated the little book into German. It was published in 1939 by Albert de Lange of Amsterdam with Anna and Sigmund Freud mentioned as its translators.

Perhaps I have given this endearing canine aspect more emphasis than it deserves. I may not forget how deeply father shared the interest of the Princess in Greek antiquities, of which she knew much. She helped father to find some of the better pieces in his collection and, in the end, she was able to help him to save some of his favourites from the Nazis.

I, personally, came into contact with Marie Bonaparte chiefly through my work at the press.

I was invited to her home in Paris and I spent holidays at her place at St Tropez.

This story is unimportant, but I cannot resist the temptation to tell of an incident at St Tropez one evening when the Princess, her children and I were dining in the open air in front of the house. The dinner was excellent; the night was cool enough to be pleasant, and a wonderful evening was going well until suddenly many thousands of ants decided to migrate from their home nest on their temporary wings in the hope of falling on suitable sites for whatever they felt impelled to do in their haphazard way. Within a few minutes they were in our hair, in our eyes, in our nostrils, down our necks, and in the soups and sauces: and all peace was disturbed. Only the Princess remained perfectly calm and rather amused, which, I think it will be admitted under the tedious circumstances, showed social genius. This was further emphasized when, capturing one of the ants, she took a powerful magnifying glass and began giving us an interesting little lecture on its wing structure during the ants' short flying stage.

At one party in a restaurant I was the only commoner, all the other guests being royal. When the waiters were at last conscious of perhaps a twinkle in my eye or some other unconscious gesture of dissent as they also addressed me as "Your Royal Highness", they dropped the "Royal" and compromised with a mere "Highness".

Because the recording of incidents during which I "walked with kings" may be misunderstood, and since it will serve to illustrate the bizarre adventures that befall people like myself on whom fate plays so many tricks, I feel bound to tell of an incident that occurred much later when I became a private in the British (Aliens) Pioneer Corps. My chief occupation was peeling potatoes when I was not scrubbing the kitchen floor. One day, through some kind of disorganization, the trays filled with sizzling sausages and onions were ready to be carried into the mess-room, but there was no one to carry them. Trying to be helpful, I took up one of the trays and made my way to the door. Here I was met by an indignant corporal who, taking the tray from my hands, barked, "Who do you think you are—to serve in the Sergeants' Mess?"

# CHAPTER XXIX

FATHER kept on his desk a kind of unbound diary in the form of large sheets of white paper upon which he recorded in a most laconic way those events of each day that seemed to him of importance. On 12th March 1938 he wrote the words "Finis Austriae", the tragic climax which began building itself up when urgent cries of newspaper sellers were heard in the usually quiet Bergasse one Saturday afternoon.

"Quick, Paula—get me the *Abend*," father called; and Paula was down the stairs and crossing the street like lightning: not that this showed particular urgency in the mind of Paula. She is still with the family, and she would still rather run than walk.

That Saturday afternoon should have been the eve of the Austrian plebiscite, a plebiscite which, we knew, never had much reality in the confused situation the Chancellor, Schuschnigg, was vainly trying to control. Indeed, we knew already that there would be no plebiscite. German troops had crossed the Austrian frontier with drums beating and flags flying; the Chancellor had resigned, and there had been disturbances even in Vienna.

But news published in the papers had seemed confused; gossip, although alarming, had to be treated as such and, in a word, we did not know what to believe.

My father at this time had begun to watch developments with eager interest, often expressing warm admiration for the brave Schuschnigg. Because the *Abend* had been a strong supporter of Austrian independence, he felt the paper Paula would bring back would give a reliable report and reduce the prevailing confusion to simple truth.

After gently taking the paper from Paula's hands, he read through the headlines and then, crumpling it in his fist, he threw it into a corner of the room. Such a scene might not be unusual in any happy land not enduring political convulsions; but father's perfect self-control seldom, or never, permitted him to show emotion: and thus all of us remained silent in the living-room, well aware that a turn of events which would allow him to fling a paper from him in disgust and disappointment must have alarming implications.

We did not dare to question him as he now sat deep in thought, thoughts which, doubtless, saw foundations crumbling and normal security fading into uncertainty; but we, too, had to know what was happening, something I sensed in the others when, after a few moments, I crossed the room and picked up the crumpled paper. The front page news, in the *Abend* of all papers, expressed jubilation: enslaved Austrians were apparently greeting liberators. Other pages were devoted to Goering, building him up as one of so much virtue, courage and wisdom that one dared to wonder, even in those tense moments, how so much that was worthy could be packed into a human being even of Goering's great girth.

All this, we knew, was bad for Austria, a tragedy indeed; but as I read through the paper, I saw that the tragedy had narrowed down for us: that we, Jews, would be the first victims. Anti-Semitic propaganda was cleverly distributed throughout the more general news items. Mean and dastardly crimes, allegedly committed by Viennese Jews, were reported and, following closely the example of Streicher's *Stuermer,* given pornographic flavour.

My own feelings, if I may express what I felt, were of horror and a strange perplexity. I, a respectable barrister and the eldest son of a man of world-wide reputation, nurtured in security and not unaffected by father's fame, I could only imagine myself enduring a nightmare, as of an innocent man standing in the dock to be condemned by judges unconcerned with a trial, and sentenced to death in dishonour.

The next day, Sunday, 13th March, the Austrian Nazis, with their band-wagons crowded with innumerable turncoats, were in full possession of Vienna. No one had offered resistance; and what resistance could there have been when it was known that a powerful German army was marching towards the capital while German bombers, cruising noisily overhead, were heralding its approach?

My own home was about five minutes' walk from my father's flat, and during those eventful days I spent most of my free time with him. The publishing press and a psychoanalytical clinic were at No. 7 Bergasse, a few doors away from father's flat. I was, of course, naturally anxious about my parents that Sunday morning, but I determined, nevertheless, to go to my office first.

Although I had urgent work to do there, I seemed unable to concentrate, I think partly because I detested the thought of the work before me as any trained lawyer would detest it: I knew that I must destroy legal documents of great importance. I had, in the course of my normal duties as a lawyer, invested money of my clients in reputable and stable currency abroad, this having been perfectly legal under lenient Austrian law; but I knew that it would be a crime in the eyes of the dollar-hungry Nazis, the punishment for which would be at least the confiscation of such funds. It was plainly my duty to protect my clients, including my father, by destroying all evidence which could lead to detection.

My adventures that Sunday morning in the office were fantastic and now seem unreal. Some days later, I might add here, the Nazi-controlled radio warned the people of Vienna against unauthorized bands of armed raiders, urging householders to detain such, and to call the police. But I could know nothing of this when such a band came to the office before I had had time to destroy any papers. As a matter of fact, I had been interrupted by the early arrival of a client, one who had now every reason to believe that certain confidential papers, neither political nor financial, which had been left in my charge were no longer safe from prying eyes. Appreciating his concern as fully justified, I had given him his documents, but although he had been as eager to go as I had been to see him depart, his natural Austrian courtesy had forced him to stay and chat for a few minutes.

Although unaware that my unwelcome visitors were hardly more than bandits whose activities were unpopular with the new authority, the fact that they were without a leader made me suspect that the raid I was enduring was an unauthorized implementation of the confused situation caused by the Nazi occupation. All their decisions were reached by majority votes, as in adventure stories written for boys. There were a dozen of them, an odd medley shabbily dressed, including a fat boy of perhaps fourteen who, nevertheless, took a full part in discussions and had a vote. The most aggressive was a small haggard-looking man who, unlike the others, who carried rifles, was armed with a revolver. At intervals throughout the incident whenever I showed no desire to co-operate, he displayed a blood-thirsty spirit by drawing his pistol and noisily pulling out and pushing in the magazine as he shouted, "Why not shoot him and be finished with him? We should shoot him on the spot."

One of the more curious aspects of this raid was the fact that across the narrow street from the office there lived a staunch Nazi who, now sitting at his open window, enjoyed a grandstand view of the proceedings: something I was unaware of at the time, otherwise, I would have drawn the curtains when an opportunity came.

Although I was held in awkward imprisonment in my office chair, two of my guards keeping their rifles pressed against my stomach for much of that Sunday, the time passed quickly enough. The antics of this crazy gang in possession of my office offered no entertainment, but a great deal happened to keep me interested. The safe had been rifled and the contents of the cash drawers, a considerable amount of money in coin and notes of a number of countries, had been placed in piles on a table, but I had removed from the safe the papers I wanted to destroy and placed them on a shelf where they had not been noticed by the raiders. My chief danger, I soon guessed, lay in the silly mind of the haggard-looking man with the revolver who, unlike the others with rifles, had live ammunition and might be controlled by an hysterical impulse if not treated carefully.

After some hours, when the initial enthusiasm of the raiders had tended to settle into something less ebullient, I asked if I might have a cup of tea. This request was instantly put to the vote, the result being indecisive until the fat boy suggested that I might be allowed to have a cup of tea provided I agreed to wash up the cup and saucer myself. This was passed with applause, but I offered an amendment to the effect that the office caretaker should be ordered to wash up the dishes. This inspired further discussion, but when it was agreed that the caretaker (who had become a Nazi without undue delay) was still my servant, I was allowed to have a cup of tea.

The unreality of my position was further emphasized when Dr Ernest Jones, a close friend of my father and now his biographer, appeared in the office. As I learnt later, he had flown from London to stand by father during these critical days. He was not permitted to speak to me, and he soon left when he saw that his only chance of helping me to escape from both a dangerous and absurd position was to appeal to a more responsible Nazi authority.

During the early part of the afternoon, the ranks of the raiders began thinning out until I was left with only one guard, a seedy-looking man of middle age whose appearance suggested an unemployed *Ober-Kellner,* a head waiter, one who would have felt happier with a napkin over his arm than with a rifle held at my stomach. Being happily ignorant of the fact that the raiders who had withdrawn had gone to my father's flat, I was relieved at this turn of events.

Now that we were alone, my guard took his rifle away from my stomach and invited me to stand up to stretch my legs, thus giving me great relief.

All this, I might say, was closely observed by the Nazi gentleman watching from the window across the street.

My guard now began a tale of woe about the hardships and privations he had had to endure in recent years and it was soon plain to me that a generous tip would be welcome. I responded at once, giving him all the money I had in my pockets, including some gold coins and a roll of notes. He was deeply grateful, so grateful in fact that I felt I might hazard a request to be allowed to visit the W.C. This was granted at once and he agreed to escort me there, a short journey across a passage which would take me past the files of documents I wanted to destroy. I managed to organize quite a number of journeys until all the papers were torn up and all had begun a procession along the elaborate Viennese sewer system.

A better conspirator than I am would have drawn the curtains while this work was in hand regardless of any one watching from across the narrow Bergasse. As it was, the Nazi gentleman observed everything, and his feelings can be imagined when he saw that during the guard's and my absences from the office when we crossed the passage to the W.C., some members of the gang returned for quick stealthy visits, to help themselves to some of the notes and coins stacked on the table. The outraged Nazi at once gave the alarm to Nazi headquarters, and the result was that within a few minutes the whole gang was back in the office, shouting and gesticulating. My guard was pinioned and searched, and my generous tip discovered. He was placed under arrest and ordered to stand in a corner.

And so the day passed until finally there arrived in a breathless condition no less a person than a *Bezirksleiter*, the District Commander of nearby S.A. headquarters, who, judging from his condition, had been running all the way. Young and of erect stature, he radiated an authority which had an immediate effect on the rabble that had been tormenting me for so long. They fell in at his sharp command and after one or two had been ordered to remain to clear up the mess in the office, the main body marched off.

The *Bezirksleiter* was correct, even polite; and I felt I was indeed awakening from a nightmare when sister Anna entered the room. She had, in fact, been waiting for some time for permission to join me. It was now I noticed a forlorn object still standing abjectly in a corner of the room, my helpful guard of the shuttle service to the W.C. The *Berzirksleiter* at once agreed to the man's release and he was even given back his rifle, but not my tip; it is certain that he would have much preferred the latter.

When one of the remaining men asked if a report should be made on the incident, the *Bezirksleiter* replied in a voice loud enough for us to hear, "Der Fall eignet sich nicht zur Weiterleitung," which, translated freely, is, "None: this case does not qualify for a report." His intention was to let us know that the sordid affair would be forgotten officially. Finally, he gave me a *passier-schein*, a pass that would permit Anna and me to accept his invitation to call at his office the next morning without danger of being stopped by ubiquitous and officious Nazi officials.

Being now free, Anna and I hurried home to Bergasse 19, being greatly relieved to know that while the raiders there had confiscated something like six thousand schillings found in father's safe, they had not behaved at all badly, being now under the control of a leader who could enforce discipline and some semblance of decent behaviour.

I think mother's attitude had had effect. Deeply concerned for father, at this time barely recovering from one of his operations and forced to spend much time resting on the sofa in his study, she called on that inner strength she shared with him, and she remained perfectly calm.

It was no small thing to a woman of mother's housewifely efficiency to see her beautifully run home invaded by a pack of irregulars. Yet she treated them as ordinary visitors, inviting them to put their rifles in the sections of the hall-stand reserved for umbrellas and even to sit down. And although the invitation was not accepted, her courtesy and courage had had a good effect. Father, too, had retained his invincible poise, leaving his sofa where he had been resting to join mother in the living-room, where he had sat calmly in his armchair throughout the raid.

Everybody's passport was confiscated, but the raid appeared to have lasted not more than an hour and a formal receipt was given for the confiscated money.

Much was due to the leader. We heard afterwards that he had been a regular field-officer in the army, one who, doubtless for economic reasons, had accepted employment by the local S.A. to train recruits. He was not a Nazi. Unfortunately for him, as it turned out, some of his men heard him addressing father respect-fully as "Herr Professor", and this, together with his correct behaviour, being duly reported, lost him his job.

When mother told father how much money had been taken from his safe he dryly remarked, "Dear me: I have never taken so much for a single visit."

In spite of this trying ordeal, I do not think father had yet any thought of leaving Austria. His intention, so far as I could judge, was to ride out the storm in the belief, shared by many civilized Europeans at this time, that the Nazi eruption was so out of step with the march of civilization, a civilization apparently supported by so many powerful democratic countries, that a normal rhythm would soon be restored and honest men permitted to go on their ways without fear.

If father had been told, even at this time, what might lie on the pathway stretching before millions of men and women of his race, what might be the fate of his elderly sisters, he would have dismissed the suggestion as fantastic.

He began to see the writing on the wall on Tuesday, 22nd March.

At one o'clock on that day, I went as usual to the Bergasse and found the flat swarming with S.S. men in smart uniforms. After a little consideration, I decided to make my visit as short as possible. There was nothing I could do to help; and the fact that I was not popular with the Nazis might even be harmful although, I have to admit, I might have been an invisible man that day judging by the way I was utterly ignored and looked through as if I were thin air; which, in fact, is not a misfortune when dealing with these people. However, before I could withdraw without arousing even slight interest, I witnessed two scenes that remain outlined on my mind. The first was the view I had from the window of Anna being driven off in an open car escorted by four heavily armed S.S. men. Her situation was perilous; but far from showing fear, or even much interest, she sat in the car as a woman might sit in a taxi on her way to enjoy a shopping expedition.

The second scene, quite as clearly outlined, is of mother, highly indignant with an S.S. man who, on his way through a passage, paused at a large cupboard, pulled open its doors and began roughly dragging out her piles of beautifully laundered linen all efficiently arranged in the way dear to her housewifely heart, each package held together by coloured ribbons.

Without showing the slightest fear, mother joined the fellow and in highly indignant tones told him precisely what she thought of his shocking behaviour in a lady's house, and ordered him to stop at once.

The S.S. man, a big fellow, jumped back from the cupboard and looked quite terrified, quickly withdrawing and appearing very sheepish indeed as mother rearranged her linen.

Father's and mother's relief when the S.S. men withdrew would have been complete had they not been so deeply anxious about Anna, who had not returned. This anxiety became acute as the day passed; but it was entirely relieved at seven o'clock that evening when at last she came home.

She had been clever enough to sense, when she had reached the Gestapo headquarters, that her chief danger lay in being left waiting in the corridor and forgotten until the office closed. In that case, she suspected, she would be swept out with other Jewish prisoners and casually deported or shot. The contempt held for the lives of Jews by the Nazis would make such an incident commonplace. Through the influence of some friends, she was allowed to leave the corridor and taken to the room where questioning of other arrested Jews was in progress. No objection was made to her presence, but this did not show any consideration for her feelings: a Jewish person was of no more account than a dog or a deaf and dumb beggar to these people, who proceeded with their questioning as if she had not been there.

But Anna was not the slightest bit deaf and she soon gathered that the Gestapo believed themselves to be hot on the scent of what they believed to be a "terror group of Jewish ex-soldiers".

I might remark that such a group did not exist; if it had existed, it is more than likely that I would have been a member.

At last Anna was questioned, being asked what it meant to be a member of an international organization, a valid question which she could answer by explaining the aims of the Psychoanalytical Association: that it was non-political and purely scientific. She was able to produce a letter addressed to her by a German member of the association, it being recognized in Germany as highly reputable. Anna was allowed to go free, but the writer of the letter was less fortunate. He had addressed her as "Sehr geehrtes gnaediges Fraeulein", the usual mode of address used between polite people; but since it had become a crime in Nazi eyes to treat a Jewish person with normal respect, his career was broken.

# CHAPTER XXX

I THINK our last sad weeks in Vienna from 11th March until the end of May would have been quite unbearable without the presence of the Princess. She had arrived in Vienna a few days after the Nazi occupation and had at once begun the magnificent work on our behalf which resulted in our rescue and that of many of father's friends. She had promised her husband, Prince George, who had not felt happy about this visit to Vienna at so dangerous a time, that she would stay at the Greek Embassy; but she spent all her days at the Bergasse with father and his family. She had been present, something I had not known until she told me, when Anna was arrested before being taken to the Gestapo headquarters. Then she had stepped forward and begged the S.S. *Sturmfuehrer* to arrest her, and take her along with Anna; but the Gestapo in Austria had not then enough courage, if it may be called courage, to risk trouble by arresting one with a royal passport. She tried by discussions with me and our lawyers to save the books of the press; but here we failed. Indeed, the Nazis were not satisfied to destroy the books remaining in Vienna; they arranged to have returned a much larger number which I had sent to Switzerland for safe keeping. The Nazi official who organized this business showed a strange sense of humour when he debited father's account with the quite considerable cost of the books' transportation to their funeral pyre in Vienna.

It was not thought advisable for me to play anything but a modest part in negotiations with the Nazis. They had forced my retirement from the Bar and, eventually, I was forbidden to enter the press offices from which they had taken away all money and documents with the assurance that everything belonging to non-Jewish clients would be returned to them. Finally I was ordered out of Vienna, a measure which could possibly have been inspired by friends who did not think my temperament sufficiently equable to be trusted: a fear I could accept as justified, so intense was my hatred of the Nazis.

My exile from the city was not hard to bear. There being no

supervision of my movements, I could go to Vienna nearly every day, to play cards with father, to discuss plans with the Princess and to help where possible in plans for the family's emigration. My mountaineering training was now of some service since I had to climb many flights of stairs: Jews were forbidden to use the lifts in public buildings.

I have a copy of the secret instruction issued by the Vienna criminal police at this time regarding the treatment of Jews. Influential well-to-do male Jews should be arrested, provided they were not too old and gave the impression of being healthy. Their property might be destroyed without interference from the ordinary police, but if it became necessary to use fire in the destruction, care should be taken that no general conflagration was started.

As father was now very old and ill, the danger of his arrest was not great, but Anna took the precaution of securing a certificate from his surgeon, a prominent Nazi, incidentally, and this made his liberty secure. As a matter of fact, no attempt to arrest father was ever made.

I was forced to leave Vienna two weeks before the others were ready to travel. During that first Sunday rag-time raid on my offices, a number of incriminating (in Nazi eyes) documents had been found and I had become a certain candidate for a concentration camp, most probably Buchenwald, where a number of my friends actually perished. Happily, the new Vice-President of Police, a man with a criminal record, was a close friend of my cook. Through this contact, I was able to buy back the documents quite cheaply and, during the negotiations, I was given timely warning of my projected arrest. Under these circumstances, it was decided that any delay in my departure might only cause embarrassment, and I decided to make for Paris to join my wife and two children, who had been sent there some days earlier.

My journey in the Ostend Express could have been uneventful, I think, had I been able to assume the normal poise of a traveller not escaping from imminent danger. There was a little wry humour in the first incident. A Jew from Rumania shared the second-class sleeper with me, and when he saw two tall blue-eyed women friends wearing swastika brooches bidding me an affectionate good-bye (many non-Nazis wore the swastika for their

own safety), the Rumanian Jew decided that he would be forced
to share the compartment with a Nazi and attempted to hide, so
far as it is possible to hide in a two-berth sleeper. I was able to
relieve his anxiety as soon as the train began moving.

I had been told that it was strictly forbidden to take any money
out of Germany, through which my train must pass, and that the
control at the frontier would be most severe. To give this warning
emphasis, I was also told that a Jew had been taken from the
train and shot in the marshalling yards because some stamps had
been found in his pocket-book. The stamps might have been
valuable issues for all the control officials knew, but, I gathered,
they hadn't worried to investigate. In view of all this, it seemed
wisest to send what bank-notes I had to a friend in Vienna
and to invest what coins I had left on food, enough to keep me
nourished until I should reach Paris and friends who would lend
me money.

When I ordered a whole roast chicken from the dining-car
attendant and asked him to keep it for me in the refrigerator until
the next morning, I filled that worthy man, who was a Nazi, with
deep suspicion. He said the unusual request was a breach of
customs regulations and that he would have to report me to the
Gestapo. Although my exit had been legally arranged through the
police, the Gestapo had not lost interest in my movements. To
avoid any further drawing of their attention, I cancelled the
request, carried the chicken to my compartment and devoured it
without pleasure, the dining-car attendant watching me from the
corridor with deep concentration.

As it turned out, there was no frontier control, the sleeping-car
attendant preventing the customs officers from entering the car
since, he explained, he did not want his passengers disturbed.

It is impossible to express the relief I felt when, at last, the train
crossed the Rhine bridge at Strasbourg and I had steamed out of
Hell into a Heaven which I felt would be entirely happy when
mother, father and Anna could join me.

And thus I pass from a story which, inevitably, I have occupied
more fully than I could wish. I conclude by telling of the family's
adventures in Vienna before they, too, gained freedom.

Father had little hope of being able to carry with him his
valuable collection of antiques; but the valuer, most probably a

secret admirer of Sigmund Freud, reached a figure a few pence under the maximum permitted for export. The commissar whom the Nazis had placed in the press with instructions to destroy it, went about his work with surprising gentleness and did all he could to protect the family from indignities. Anna discovered that he had studied chemistry under Professor Hertzig, one of the few Jewish lecturers in Vienna and a close friend of father's. The commissar treated father with great reverence and was greatly shocked one day when an S.S. man pushed him roughly aside as he was knocking at the door of father's study. "Kamerad," he snapped, "wir klopfen nicht an! (We do not knock at doors)."

This was when an S.S. party had come to ask father to give a certificate proclaiming that he had been well treated by the authorities. Without hesitation, father wrote, "Ich kann die Gestapo jedermann auf das beste empfeh len (I can recommend the Gestapo very much to everyone)", using the style of a commercial advertisement: irony that escaped the Nazis, although they were not altogether sure as they passed the certificate from man to man. Finally, however, they shrugged their shoulders and marched off, evidently deciding that it was the best the old man could think of.

Father had to say good-bye to his old sisters. He and his brother Alexander had supplied them with ample means to live in comfort for the rest of their lives; but I have already told of their fate. A last attempt to rescue them with the help of the Princess failed after she had secured them an entry permit into France.

Uncle Alexander managed to escape after he had been thoroughly robbed by the Nazis. He joined father in London for a time before going to Canada.

One of the humiliations suffered in Vienna by those Jewish people who had gained permission to leave was a daily visit to the police. When sister Anna returned from the Gestapo office with all the release papers safely in her hands, she told father of this condition. "You, Anna," he said, "have of course refused to obey so humiliating an order."

This remark shows father's defiant spirit; but Anna knew that any one who dared to refuse to obey a demand made in the Hotel Metropole, the headquarters of the Gestapo, would not leave its dreaded doors alive and free.

218

On 24th May, my sister Mathilde and her husband left, reaching London without incident, and at last, on 2nd June, the *Unbedenklichkeitserklaerung*, the declaration that there was no objection, was issued: the price demanded for Sigmund Freud's release had been paid by the Princess, whom my father repaid as soon as he had regained his freedom.

The next day, father, mother, Anna and father's dog left for Paris, where they were welcomed by the Princess, and a day later they reached England. All was at last well for all, except the dog: she had to spend six months in quarantine. England gave father a warm welcome, many of the papers expressing satisfaction that a man of Sigmund Freud's importance in the world was making his home in London.

Father's feelings are best expressed in this extract from a letter he wrote to my brother Ernst just before leaving Vienna:

"Two prospects present themselves in these troubled times—to see you all together once more, and to die in freedom. Sometimes I see myself as a Jacob being taken by his children to Egypt when he was very old. Let us hope that there will not follow an exodus from Egypt. It is time that Ahasver comes to rest somewhere."

I end my story with the words spoken by Ernest Jones at father's cremation:

"He died surrounded by every loving care in a land that had shown him more courtesy, more esteem and more honour than had his own or any other country, a land which, I think, he himself esteemed beyond all others."

I can add that Ernest Jones was right. Father loved England.